D1438602

MW
DP1000129910
KFINE

Simon Starling

Simon Starling

Recent History

CAC MÁLAGA
CENTRO DE ARTE CONTEMPORÁNEO DE MÁLAGA

26 NOVIEMBRE 2010 - 23 ENERO 2011
26 NOVEMBER 2010 - 23 JANUARY 2011

TATE St IVES

5 FEBRERO - 2 MAYO 2011
5 FEBRUARY - 2 MAY 2011

cacmálaga
Centro de Arte Contemporáneo

Ayuntamiento
de Málaga

Índice | **Contents**

MÁLAGA da la bienvenida a Simon Starling, uno de los artistas conceptuales británicos más destacados del panorama internacional, que presenta en el CAC Málaga su primera exposición individual en un museo de arte español desde que obtuviera el prestigioso *Turner Prize* en 2005.

Su obra es fruto de largos procesos de investigación, de continuas transformaciones de la materia y de una cuidada atención a los procesos de creación. Simon Starling es un artista comprometido con la historia de las instituciones de arte en las que expone su obra. Quizás por dicha razón, para su exposición en el CAC Málaga el artista trabaja con la arquitectura del edificio con un proyecto *site specific*, en el que deja al descubierto el pasado del mismo como Mercado de Mayoristas reconvertido ahora en centro de arte de vanguardia.

Quiero agradecer el apoyo y la confianza que la TATE St Ives ha depositado en el Ayuntamiento de Málaga al colaborar con el CAC Málaga en este importante proyecto, siendo la primera vez que esta prestigiosa organización internacional acoge un intercambio con un centro de arte español.

Desde aquí animo a todos los malagueños y visitantes a descubrir la propuesta expositiva de Simon Starling en Málaga, una gran oportunidad de conocer la obra de uno de los artistas más reputados. Una vez más, la ciudad pone de manifiesto su compromiso y su apuesta firme por convertirse en punto de encuentro internacional en el mundo del arte y de la cultura.

FRANCISCO DE LA TORRE PRADOS | ALCALDE DE MÁLAGA

LA OBRA del británico Simon Starling posee la extraordinaria capacidad de trasladarnos a otro mundo, un mundo reescrito por él mismo en el que se adentra en las posibilidades formales de los objetos. Simon Starling no parece satisfecho con la relación que la sociedad y los seres humanos establecen con los objetos, de ahí su interés por conferirles un nuevo sentido: Starling recodifica la realidad presente en lo que parece una búsqueda constante del origen natural de los elementos.

El trabajo de Starling se centra en la transformación de la materia, es una reflexión sobre la identidad de las cosas y el significado de las mismas. Los objetos cotidianos, las cosas e instrumentos que invaden nuestro entorno, son el punto de partida creativo de su trabajo que, tras un minucioso proceso de investigación, viajes en solitario y el establecimiento de conexiones culturales e históricas, dan paso a un juego visual y conceptual del que se desprende una disconformidad con la alienación provocada por el capitalismo y la globalización.

Una idea fundamental que domina todo su trabajo creativo es que sus obras no son entes sencillos sino algo más intangible compuesto por una suerte de objetos, textos, imágenes, libros e, incluso, lecturas, asesorías técnicas y conversaciones. Una profunda investigación para saber cómo funcionan las cosas y, a su vez, darles un nuevo uso o recuperar del olvido aquéllas que han sido desechadas por el progreso y las nuevas tecnologías. Las creaciones de Simon Starling representan un afán constante, una preocupación insistente y casi obsesiva, por reubicar el pasado en el presente. Este proceso le permite, además, plantear interrogantes sobre los valores culturales, el medioambiente y la economía global. La búsqueda del origen justifica su preocupación por el proceso de producción de sus obras y por trasladar al espectador el problema de cómo la producción masiva está relegando indefectiblemente a las técnicas artesanales y, por tanto, de alguna manera, está limitando la capacidad imaginativa del ser humano y su identidad como el ser creativo natural. El CAC Málaga con este proyecto presenta la primera exposición individual en España de Simon Starling tras recibir el *Turner Prize* en 2005, que itinerará a la Tate St Ives, gracias al acuerdo de colaboración de intercambio de exposiciones entre ambas instituciones, donde el proyecto del CAC Málaga será recodificado en el contexto del Cornwall rural, donde también se creará una nueva obra *site specific*.

Esta exposición de Simon Starling es el resultado de un cuidado proceso en el que el visitante no debe limitarse a contemplar el resultado final sino que lo anima a adentrarse y a conocer la historia que ha ocasionado esta transformación y construcción de la materia.

Sirvan estas últimas líneas para agradecer el trabajo y la dedicación de todas las personas implicadas en la organización de la exposición y en la elaboración del catálogo, así como nuestra gratitud a Simon Starling y a sus galeristas por su interés e implicación en este proyecto del CAC Málaga, desarrollado en colaboración con la Tate St Ives.

FERNANDO FRANCÉS | DIRECTOR, CAC MÁLAGA

MARTIN CLARK | DIRECTOR ARTÍSTICO, TATE St IVES

MÁLAGA would like to welcome Simon Starling, one of the leading British conceptual artists on the international art scene. The present exhibition at the CAC Málaga is the first solo show of his work to be held in a Spanish museum since he won the prestigious Turner Prize in 2005.

Simon Starling's work arises from lengthy investigative procedures, continuous transformations of material and a painstaking focus on creative processes. He is an artist committed to the history of the institutions in which he exhibits his creations. Perhaps for this reason, for the present exhibition at the CAC Málaga he has focused on the architecture of the building itself through a site-specific project that uncovers the building's past and its previous function as a wholesale market, now transformed into a contemporary art centre.

I would like to thank the Tate St Ives for the support and confidence it has shown towards the City Council of Málaga, manifested in its involvement in this important project of the CAC Málaga. This is the first time that this prestigious international institution has participated in an exhibition exchange with a Spanish art centre.

I would like to encourage all local residents and visitors to see this exhibition in Málaga of the work of Simon Starling, offering as it does an outstanding opportunity to discover the work of one of the leading names in contemporary art. Once again the city of Málaga has revealed its firm commitment to becoming an international meeting point within the world of art and culture.

FRANCISCO DE LA TORRE PRADOS | MAYOR OF MÁLAGA

THE WORK of the British artist Simon Starling possesses the remarkable ability to transport us to another world: a world re-written by the artist himself in which he investigates the formal potential of objects. Starling seems dissatisfied with the relationship that society and human beings establish with objects, hence his interest in endowing them with new meaning. He re-codifies today's reality in what seems to be an ongoing quest for the natural origin of things.

Starling's work focuses on the transformation of material and is a reflection on the identity of things and their meaning. The everyday objects, things and devices that invade our surroundings constitute the creative starting point for his work in which, following painstaking research, travels and a process of establishing cultural and historical connections, a visual and conceptual game emerges that expresses dissent with the alienation provoked by capitalism and globalisation.

Pervading all of Starling's work is the fundamental idea that his creations are not simple realities but rather something more intangible made up of a combination of objects, texts, images and books, in addition to talks, technical recommendations and conversations. It is, in short, a profound investigative process that aims to discover how things works and to equip them with new uses or to revive forgotten, obsolete ones that have been cast aside by progress and new technologies. Simon Starling's creations involve a permanent desire to locate the past in the present, expressed through an insistent, almost obsessive interest. This process also allows him to raise questions about cultural values, the environment and the global economy. His quest for origins explains his interest in the process of production of his work and in his desire to convey to the viewer the problem of how mass production is irrevocably relegating craft techniques to oblivion, thus limiting our imaginative powers and our identities as natural creative beings.

The exhibition at the CAC Málaga is the first solo show of the work of Simon Starling in Spain since he was awarded the Turner Prize in 2005. It has been conceived to travel to Tate St Ives – as part of a reciprocal exhibition exchange established between the two institutions – where it will be re-presented in the very different context of rural Cornwall, and where a major new site specific work will be created.

Underlying this exhibition is a painstaking process that encourages the visitor not only to contemplate the final result but also to enter into and learn about the narrative that has brought about this transformation and creation of material.

We would like to take this opportunity to thank all those involved in the organisation of the exhibition and the preparation of the catalogue, as well as to express our gratitude to Simon Starling and his gallerists for their interest and involvement in this project initiated by the CAC Málaga and developed in association with Tate St Ives.

FERNANDO FRANCÉS I DIRECTOR, CAC MÁLAGA

MARTIN CLARK I ARTISTIC DIRECTOR, TATE St IVES

Vistas de la exposición / Installation views *Simon Starling. Recent History*, CAC Málaga, 2010

1:1, 1:10; 1:100, 2010

Historia reciente. Narrativas sumergidas

MONTSE BADIA

EL TRABAJO de Simon Starling consiste en una intensa búsqueda que comprende viajes, investigación y la posibilidad de realizar conexiones entre diferentes lugares, objetos y circunstancias históricas y culturales. Los planteamientos de Starling, tan humorísticos como eruditos, acostumbran a ser peculiares. Desarrolla proyectos específicos, en relación a contextos determinados. Sus viajes –que son tanto o más importantes como el destino o el resultado final– revelan relaciones escondidas, narrativas sumergidas, historias en proceso de transformación de un objeto o sustancia en otro. Contrapone literal y metafóricamente diferentes estructuras y dinámicas. Revela conexiones entre tiempos y lugares distintos. Sus investigaciones son, como su propia etimología indica, recorridos "en pos de una huella" o "en busca de una pista". En su pensamiento y en sus procesos de trabajo un paso sigue a otro, un descubrimiento lleva a una nueva conexión. Como en un laboratorio, el margen de error forma parte del propio proceso. Como en una reacción en cadena, se crean nuevas referencias o nuevas relaciones que contribuyen a maneras diferentes de mirar, pensar y actuar.

Y al final de toda investigación aparece el relato. Starling es un investigador, un viajero y también un narrador. Los textos y libros que acompañan sus obras forman parte intrínseca de éstas. Las informaciones que aporta son esenciales para poder acercarnos al proceso y a las conexiones que establece. La relación entre narración y escultura es constantemente renegociada y explorada. Así, las narraciones acompañan a obras de una fuerte presencia en el espacio expositivo. Sus proyectos adoptan la forma de instalaciones, de objetos elegantemente fabricados, de fotografías, filmes o libros. Starling combina y baraja las estrategias técnicas y conceptuales de la misma manera que juega con todo el bagaje cultural que tiene a sus espaldas.

Cambios de escala

Las exposiciones que Simon Starling presenta en el Centro de Arte Contemporáneo de Málaga y en la Tate St Ives comparten un mismo punto de partida: una intervención directa en la arquitectura de las instituciones para, a continuación, articular un grupo de trabajos que giran en torno a las ideas de cambio de escala, de miniaturización y de magnificación, así como de transferencia de datos en una forma física o escultórica y viceversa, la traducción de formas reales de datos. Ambas exposiciones son complementarias y en ambos casos la relación con el lugar se ve alterado. La noción de historia también desempeña un papel importante cuando nos referimos a las recientes historias políticas y arquitectónicas en el caso de las nuevas obras creadas para el CAC Málaga, y a los antiguos recursos geológicos que constituyeron la base económica de Cornwall como región minera, al igual que la historia cultural más inmediata del pueblo de St. Ives como colonia internacional de arte modernista.

En la Tate St Ives, Starling empieza confrontando dos instituciones muy distintas y distantes, al introducir en el edificio de la Tate una copia a escala 1:1 del espacio de exposiciones del Pier Arts Centre en Orkney, Escocia. Tanto la Tate St Ives como el Pier Arts Centre dan al mar, la primera en la punta más septentrional de las Islas Británicas y el segundo en la parte más al oeste. Ambas instituciones guardan una intensa relación con la colonia de artistas del siglo XX en St. Ives.[1] Hace un par de años, Starling mostró su obra de diapositivas *Autoxylopyrocycloboros* (2006) en el Pier Arts Centre. Para este trabajo, navegó por el Loch Long en Escocia, en un pequeño barco de vapor "customizado" que se alimentaba de la propia madera del barco, hasta que finalmente quedó reducido a la mínima expresión y se hundió. Por una parte, esta pieza se inspira en la cultura de protesta de la zona contra los submarinos nucleares, puesto que son abundantes en esas mismas aguas. Por otra, la obra constituye una buena muestra del humor, cercano a los dibujos animados

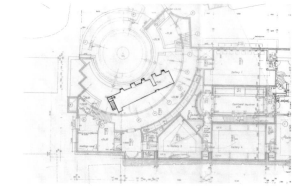

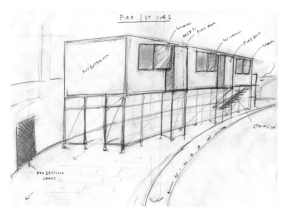

Simon Starling
Reconstrucción del espacio del Pier Art Centre Gallery /
Reconstruction of Pier Art Centre Gallery space

de Tom y Jerry o del artista danés Peter Land.[2] La reconstrucción de la galería Orkney en la Tate crea una fusión espectacular de estos dos espacios dispares, y la sala reproducida –en el espacio curvo, con cristalera, de la galería Tate St Ives– aparece como una especie de barco en una botella. La obra sigue la senda de otras esculturas arquitectónicas que Starling ha realizado en los últimos años y que a menudo regresan a una narrativa o relato histórico, pero en este caso casi representa y reinvestiga literalmente un pedazo de su propia "historia reciente". *Autoxylopyrocycloboros* se vuelve a instalar en el espacio, exactamente como antes, acompañada ahora por otra obra, un cuadro de un barco a vapor pintado por el pescador y artista de St. Ives Alfred Wallis. Realizado en St. Ives hacia 1934, el cuadro ahora forma parte de la colección del Pier Arts Centre, y volverá a St. Ives dentro del "casco" del espacio reproducido de la galería, a la deriva respecto a su sitio habitual. De esta manera, se crea una especie de narrativas sumergidas, de doble bucle en el que todos los elementos y situaciones aparecen relacionados.

La obra central de la exposición en Málaga, *1:1, 1:10, 1:100* (2010) trabaja a partir de la propia realidad del edificio que acoge el museo, el antiguo Mercado de Mayoristas, una construcción de líneas rectas y cuerpos cúbicos, que respeta la forma triangular del solar. Si la sala principal de exposiciones subraya la forma triangular de la planta del museo, Starling redunda en este aspecto, al mostrar una maqueta parcial del museo. Por un lado, el artista presenta dentro del espacio, una maqueta a menor escala del centro. Por otro lado, propone la realización de una nueva, pero esta vez utilizando materiales extraídos de la propia construcción del museo, retirados de algunos muros para hacer posible esta construcción. La idea de utilizar los propios muros del museo es, tal como el artista comentaba en una conversación el pasado mes de octubre, *"una manera de desnudar el nuevo museo para revelar la arquitectura de tipo fascista de finales de los años 30 que esconde debajo. No es más que una manera lúdica de hablar de la amnesia inducida por los nuevos muros y paneles que cubren la fachada frontal del museo"*.

La nueva maqueta realizada por Starling acoge otra maqueta del museo, que no es visible, sino que se encuentra "encerrada en la nueva maqueta", casi enterrada como si se

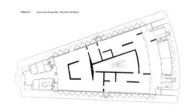

Plano del CAC Málaga / CAC Málaga floor plan
con / with *1:1, 1:10, 1:100* (2010)

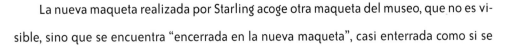

tratara de un mausoleo. Como si de un juego de muñecas rusas se tratara, se crea un espacio híbrido entre el modelo y la propia arquitectura, de manera que el museo acoge su maqueta y, al mismo tiempo, genera otra a partir de sus propios materiales, en una suerte de bucle de escalas, materiales y funcionalidades diferentes. Como recordaba Sean Lynch en un texto con motivo de la exposición que Simon Starling presentó en Limerick[3] el trabajo de Simon guarda relación con los planteamientos de los protagonistas del libro *The Third Policemen* (1967) de Flann O'Brien. El libro, que de alguna forma se relaciona con la teoría de los átomos (entre otras, sigue la teoría atómica que postula la hibridación progresiva del ciclista y la bicicleta por cambio de materia), cuenta con una serie de personajes bastante peculiares que van desde un científico excéntrico, hasta un condenado a muerte, para hablar de la forma en que el mundo es construido, deconstruido o reconstruido. Uno de esos personajes, un policía que hace de artesano en su tiempo libre, construye una pequeña caja de madera que contiene otra exactamente igual y así sucesivamente hasta veintinueve, de las cuales sólo trece son visibles.

Maqueta del CAC Málaga escala 1:100 escondida en *1:1, 1:10, 1:100* (2010) / CAC Málaga architecture model scale 1:100 hidden inside *1:1, 1:10, 1:100* (2010)

Gestos de modificación

A partir de este trabajo en relación a los edificios del CAC Málaga y de la Tate St Ives, sigue un conjunto de obras centradas en la noción de partículas o átomos que trabajan a partir de la idea de transferencia de los datos o los códigos de una imagen en una forma física o escultórica y viceversa. Es el caso de *Particle Projection (Loop)* (2007). Como en la mayoría de trabajos de Simon Starling, el punto de partida se basa en el contexto. En este caso, el proyecto fue pensado con motivo de la inauguración del centro de arte Wiels, en Bruselas, ubicado en una antigua destilería. Para ello, Starling tomó dos referencias de la cultura belga que, como es habitual en él, acabaron conectándose: un edificio paradigmático de los años 50 y un artista fundamental pionero de toda una corriente de prácticas artísticas posteriores basadas en la "crítica institucional". Con todas estas referencias, tomadas como material de trabajo, el artista produce una nueva imagen de una tecnología a punto de desaparecer.

Las referencias y sus conexiones constituyen en sí mismas una historia que es fundamental explicar aquí. En el año 1957, el artista Marcel Broodthaers trabajó como obrero en el edificio del Atomium, diseñado por André Waterkeyn para la Feria Internacional de Bruselas del año 1958. La arquitectura del edificio es una representación esquemática de un cristal de metal, el símbolo abstracto del concepto de átomo. Broodthaers registró la construcción del pabellón mediante una serie de fotografías, más tarde publicadas en el periódico *Le Patriote Illustré*. Cuando cincuenta años después de su construcción, el edificio del Atomium fue restaurado, sustituyendo el aluminio envejecido por nuevos paneles triangulares, se hizo una serie de fotografías en blanco y negro que reproducían exactamente las que en su día había realizado Broodthaers. En un laboratorio químico berlinés, se tomó uno de los negativos de las fotografías que documentaban la restauración del Atomium. El negativo fue despojado de su capa de gel, con lo que las partículas de plata del revelado quedaron al descubierto. Bajo un microscopio electrónico, los fragmentos de estas partículas presentaban una apariencia esponjosa y fantasmal y configuran un tipo diferente de "arquitectura", poblada de estructuras laberínticas en constante mutación. Una de esas partículas fue devuelta de nuevo a la película fotográfica, pero en este caso notablemente ampliada, lo que le otorga ciertas connotaciones espectrales.

Particle Projection (Loop) se puede mostrar tanto como proyección o como objeto en forma de instalación en dos vitrinas, con la película en 35 milímetros y los contactos ampliados de las fotografías originales, que evidencian esta idea de bucle. En este sentido, Starling concibe sus trabajos no tanto como un elemento singular, sino más bien como una constelación de objetos, textos, imágenes, libros o incluso charlas, que de alguna manera están vinculados al cuerpo del trabajo.

Traducciones morfológicas. El caso Moore

La traducción es otra noción clave para Starling. Cercano a la visión "on translation" del artista Antoni Muntadas, transforma o traduce una cosa en otra, del lenguaje a los códigos, de la ciencia a la tecnología, de lo visible a lo invisible... Y, sobre todo, le interesa lo que sucede en el proceso, lo que cambia, lo que se pierde y lo que aparece, las relaciones que se establecen. Siguiendo con la idea de la transferencia de datos, *Project for a Meeting (Chicago)* (2010) es un nuevo trabajo en el que el artista retoma su interés por la obra de Henry Moore, uno de los escultores emblemáticos del movimiento moderno. Las alusiones y referencias a la modernidad son habituales en los proyectos de Starling. Por un lado, como evidencia del fracaso de las utopías y, por otro, como recuperación de aquel impulso nostálgico. *Project for a Meeting (Chicago)* consiste en una serie de tres uranotipos y forma parte de una investigación sobre la historia de dos esculturas muy similares de Henry Moore, *Atom Piece* y *Nuclear Energy*, que existen en dos contextos muy contradictorios: el lugar donde se creó el primer reactor nuclear, en la Universidad de Chicago, es decir, los inicios del llamado Proyecto Manhattan para desarrollar las primeras bombas atómicas para ser utilizadas en tiempos de guerra, y el Hiroshima City Museum of Contemporary Art, en Hiroshima, ciudad que padeció las nefastas consecuencias de la bomba atómica. La serie de tres imágenes creadas por Starling propone una reunión ficticia entre estas dos obras casi idénticas, a excepción de su tamaño. Para cerrar este círculo de relaciones, los uranotipos han sido realizados mediante un proceso de revelado, ya casi olvidado, cuyo principal ingrediente es un compuesto de óxido de uranio.

La relación entre *Atom Piece* y *Nuclear Energy* es significativa. *Atom Piece* fue un modelo de trabajo para *Nuclear Energy*. El propio Moore explicaba como le llegó el proyecto: "*aunque suene extraño yo tuve la idea para esta escultura antes de que el Profesor McNeill y sus colegas de la Universidad de Chicago vinieran a verme un domingo por la mañana para hacerme la propuesta. Me explicaron (algo que yo conocía vagamente) que Fermi, el físico nuclear italiano, hizo sus primeros experimentos con éxito de fisión nuclear controlada en un edificio provisional. Creo que era un edificio de madera, que desde fuera no parecía en absoluto que estuviera albergando algo de tanta importancia. El experimento fue llevado a cabo en secreto y tener éxito significaba que el hombre era capaz de controlar una fuerza enorme tanto con una finalidad pacífica como destructiva. Vinieron a mi y me dijeron que pensaban que el lugar en el que un acontecimiento tan importante tuvo lugar debía ser señalado y me preguntaron si quería hacer una escultura para ese lugar".*[4]

Esta no es la primera vez que Starling se interesa por el trabajo y la figura de Henry Moore. En *Silver Particle/Bronze (After Henry Moore)* (2008), toma una foto pequeña en blanco y negro, registrada por el propio Moore de su escultura *Reclining Figure No. 4*. A partir de ahí, hace un corte circular en la fotografía, extrayendo la imagen de una de las partículas de plata. El detalle fue escaneado y manipulado hasta conseguir un modelo en 3D que fue traducido en forma de escultura que finalmente mostraba un aspecto muy parecido a las del escultor británico. De hecho, el método de trabajo del propio Moore consistía en realizar pequeños modelos que sus asistentes ampliaban hasta conseguir sus características esculturas.

El paso de fotografía a escultura a partir de una cadena de reproducción, remite a la materialidad de la obra, puesto que considera la fotografía no sólo por su valor como imagen, soporte de memoria o documento, sino también como receptáculo de partículas metálicas o, como el artista ha comentado en alguna ocasión, *"como un campo de esculturas potenciales".*

El interés de Starling en Moore tiene que ver sin duda con su condición de escultor de la modernidad, pero también con su investigación acerca de las instituciones artísticas. En *Project for a Masquerade (Hiroshima)* (2010) un trabajo que forma parte de la exposición en tres partes que el artista está desarrollando para The Modern Institute de Glasgow, Hiroshima City Museum of Contemporary Art y The Gallery of Modern Art de Edimburgo, Starling profundiza en el estudio de las conexiones entre Moore y la Guerra Fría. *Project for a Masquerade* consiste en la presentación de nueve personajes, protagonistas de *Eboshiori*, una obra de teatro tradicional japonés Noh. Seis de los personajes están representados por una máscara realizada en madera; dos de ellos por máscaras de bronce y uno por un sombrero. La obra narra la historia de un joven noble que con la ayuda de un fabricante de sombreros, se disfraza para escapar y empezar una nueva vida en el este del Japón. En esta historia de reinvención personal, Starling sitúa a personas del entorno de Moore, en el contexto de la Guerra Fría, para hablar de la doble vida de *Atom Piece*, que nació como una escultura autónoma que más tarde sirvió de modelo para *Nuclear Energy* y tuvo que cambiar de nombre, entre otras cosas, porque la palabra "piece" del título podía confundirse con "peace", un vocablo en las antípodas del contexto nuclear y de Guerra Fría.

Los protagonistas de *Project for a Masquerade (Hiroshima)* son, entre otros, Henry Moore, que es el fabricante de sombreros; Enrico Fermi como el mensajero; Joseph Hirshorn como Kumasaka, un bandido oportunista; James Bond como el mercader de oro; Anthony Blunt como la mujer del sombrerero y Atom Piece-Nuclear Energy como Ushikawa, el joven noble. La mezcla de personajes reales y fictícios o que el protagonista sea una escultura, así como el rol femenino otorgado a Anthony Blunt no dejan de ser rasgos del fino sentido del humor del artista. Anteriormente Starling había realizado conexiones entre Moore y la Guerra Fría al analizar su relación con Anthony Blunt, un doble agente que trabajó para la NKVD de la Unión Soviética y para el M15 del gobierno británico. Blunt fue también bien conocido en el mundo del arte por su papel como profesor de historia del arte en la Universidad de Londres, crítico de arte, defensor del trabajo de Moore, y director del Courtauld Institute of Art de Londres. Con las obras *Project for a Meeting (Chicago)* y *Project for a Masquerade (Hiroshima)*, Starling analiza el papel de Moore como autor del homenaje al padre de la energía nuclear, sin olvidar que Moore fue uno de los patrocinadores públicos de la Campaña por el Desarme Nuclear. Rizando aún más el rizo, por ese mismo periodo Moore vendió una cincuentena de esculturas a Joseph Hirshhorn –un empresario y coleccionista que se definía como "Mr. Oportunidad"– que hizo su fortuna en el negocio del petróleo, la venta de oro y las perspectivas de uranio en Canadá en los 60.

La existencia física de la fotografía

En otra obra reciente, *300:1 (After Wilhelm Wagenfeld)* (2010) Starling vuelve al interés por la fotografía como receptor de sentido y también como elemento del que explorar su existencia física a partir de los elementos que forman las imágenes, que son presentados en 3D. La obra consiste en una serie de bolas de cristal negro soplado, una serie de impresiones *offset* y alfileres para colgar las fotografías. Las imágenes muestran objetos de vidrio diseñados por la bauhaus, inspirados en diseños del movimiento moderno. El tamaño de las bolas de cristal se corresponde con el de los puntos de las perforaciones de los alfileres que sujetan las imágenes en la pared. Este trabajo surge como consecuencia de una gran instalación realizada por el artista en Pouges-les-Eaux, Francia, en el año 2009 y que tenía por título *La Source (demi-teinte)*. Originariamente en ese lugar, que era un antiguo emplazamiento

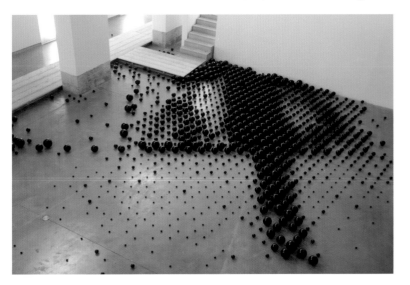

balneario, se embotellaba agua de propiedades especiales. En su instalación *La Source*, Starling colocó una caja de luz que mostraba una reproducción ampliada de una fotografía de principios del siglo XX en el que podía verse el suelo del edificio en el que ahora exponía, cubierto de filas ordenadas de botellas. Al fondo de la imagen podían verse los trabajadores. El artista hizo un recorte circular en la imagen, creando. Ya dentro del edificio, construyó una pasarela que recorría uno de los estrechos pasillos, mientras una serie de rampas conectaban las pasarelas con las escaleras que conducían a las salas superiores. Sobre el suelo de hormigón gris, se distribuían 1036 esferas de cristal negro hechas a mano en seis tamaños distintos. El efecto era de una gran red que reflejaba de manera distorsionada la arquitectura del propio edificio. La conexión entre las bolas de cristal negro y la imagen original era tan directa como remota: el círculo que el artista recortó de la fotografía, fue ampliado a la escala del

Simon Starling
La Source (demi-teinte), 2009
Exposición / Exhibition *Simon Starling. THEREHERETHENTHERE (la Source)*,
Parc Saint Léger, Centre d'art contemporain de Pogues-les Eaux, 2009
Foto / Photo: Aurélien Mole

edificio, de manera que cada uno de los puntos de impresión fue "traducido" en sus co-rrespondientes bolas de cristal negro. Observado desde el balcón superior, las esferas podían leerse como secciones de dos de las botellas y un fragmento del suelo, de la imagen de la caja de luz.

Si *La Source* fue un proyecto extremadamente complejo *300:1 (After Wilhelm Wagenfeld)* se presenta como una escala menor del mismo proyecto, que alude de una manera más precisa al ambiguo espacio entre la manufactura en masa y el trabajo único y artesanal.

Piedras, evolución y difusión

En el caso de *Archaeopteryx Litographica* (2008), las conexiones se realizan entre las teorías de la evolución y un tipo de tecnología de reproducción que contribuyó a la difusión de las primeras. La obra consiste en dos elementos complementarios: una escultura y un conjunto de impresiones de plata. La escultura, "Archaeopteryx Lithographica", toma su nombre de uno de los fósiles más importantes encontrados en la historia. Con esta obra, Starling explora un momento clave en el siglo XIX en el que la intensificación de la impresión *offset* tuvo una gran incidencia en la difusión de las teorías de la evolución que mediante el fósil encontrado habían podido establecer una relación entre los dinosaurios y las aves.

Archaeopteryx se convierte así en una serie litográfica compuesta por seis litografías que encadena las diversas realidades de la imagen: la reproducción litográfica de la fotografías del texto, la fotografía de la litografía

Simon Starling
Archaeopteryx Lithographica, 2008-2009
Foto / Photo: Jens Ziehe

de los fósiles de piedra litográfica, la impresión litográfica de la fotografía de los fósiles, etc.

Viajes a través de la historia y la técnica

Siguiendo con esta idea transferir datos de un medio a otro, incluso de una dimensión a otra, cabe destacar la pieza *D1-Z1 (22,686,575:1)*, (2009). El trabajo hace referencia a la que fue considerada como la primera computadora programable del mundo, la Z1 que fue diseñada en 1936 por el ingeniero y artista Konrad Zuse (1910-1995) y ocupaba toda una habitación. Con 172 bytes de memoria y capacidad para sumar, restar, multiplicar y dividir, la Z1 fue financiada de manera privada y literalmente fabricada en casa de los padres de Zuse en Berlín. Completado en 1938 el equipo fue "programado" con alimentación de cinta perforada en un lector. Zuse grabó sus programas en película fotográfica de 35 mm.

D1- Z1 muestra una secuencia de 30 segundos en la que se ve la imagen de la propia maquinaria en acción. Como es habitual en Starling, la laboriosidad que acompaña sus procesos de trabajo parece en ocasiones descomunal para los resultados que se obtienen y, en otras ocasiones, parecen simplemente acercarse a una crítica a la presión por la efectividad y la economía del tiempo actuales. De este modo, las imágenes de *D1 - Z1 (22,686,575:1)* se generaron utilizando tecnología de animación, incluyendo programas de renderización producidos en Berlín. La generación de esta simple secuencia de 30 segundos de animación, que representa el lector de películas perforadas (una pequeña parte de la gran máquina), requiere 3.992.837,240 bytes de información, es decir, más de 22 millones de veces la memoria de la Z1. Esta reconstrucción virtual generada por ordenador, se transfirió luego a una película de 35 mm y fue exhibida en otra pieza representativa de la tecnología alemana de mediados de siglo, un proyector Dresde D1, modificado para poder proyectar en bucle. En la imagen proyectada que aparece con una cierta indefinición, se muestra la propia maquinaria en acción, con la película moviéndose a través de la máquina. Tan hipnótico como formalista, el trabajo no deja de ser un homenaje a la perseverancia de Zuse, muy cercana a la del propio Starling, sin esconder una aproximación un tanto humorística a una manera de hacer bien lejana de la actual. De hecho, todas estas máquinas o técnicas recogidos en estos proyectos, desde el ordenador de Zuse hasta los revelados con uranio o la manera artesanal de trabajar el vidrio durante el período moderno son utilizados por el artista como elementos para reflexionar sobre una realidad contemporánea, que se nos presenta mucho más desmaterializada.

De esta manera, Starling realiza un viaje entre dos contextos, históricos y técnicos. Combina la alta tecnología con la baja tecnología, para producir una imagen del primer prototipo de calculadora programable. El interés de Starling en la imagen parte de la relación que puede establecer con la máquina que la reproduce, con una voluntad de mostrar el dispositivo, lo que éste representa y sus connotaciones históricas y sociales.

Al igual que otro trabajo anterior, *Wilhelm Noak oHG* (2006) —en el que una película en 35 mm proyecta la construcción de una escalera, mientras la película física se va enrollando alrededor de esta misma escalera–, *D1-Z1 (22,686,575:1)* documenta su modo de fabricación. En ambos casos, reencontramos el bucle en relación a la historia de la técnica y al soporte en película, que se actualizan en un espacio cargado de nuevas implicaciones.

Simon Starling
Rough-Cut Block of Belgian Black Marble
Catella Marmi, Moncalieri, Italy, 2008
Exposición / Exposition *Three Birds, Seven Stories,*
Interpolations and Bifurcations, 2008. Galleria Franco Noero, Turín / Turin

Simon Starling
1:1 scale model of the 5th Floor of 9 Via Giulia di Barolo, Turin
(La Fetta di Polenta) built at Uferstrasse 8, Berlin, 2008
Exposición / Exposition *Three Birds, Seven Stories,*
Interpolations and Bifurcations, 2008. Galleria Franco Noero, Turín / Turin

Simon Starling
Ballroom Doors, Manik Bagh Palace,
Indore (closed), 2008
Exposición / Exposition *Three Birds, Seven Stories,*
Interpolations and Bifurcations, 2008
Galleria Franco Noero, Turín / Turin

Seis grados de separación

El proceso de trabajo de Starling, en el que se va estableciendo una cadena de relaciones, que a priori parecerían inimaginables, entronca con la teoría propuesta en el relato *Chains* (1929) del escritor húngaro Frigyes Karinthy, y popularizada en una obra teatral de John Guare, basada en la idea de que cualquier persona del mundo puede estar conectada a cualquier otra a través de una cadena de conocidos que no tiene más de cinco intermediarios. Los seis grados de separación con los que trabaja Starling no conectarían únicamente personas, sino también hechos, situaciones y descubrimientos.

Three Birds, Seven Stories, Interpolations and Bifurcations (2008), que cuenta la historia de un arquitecto europeo al que el Maharajah de India le encargó llevar a cabo un ambicioso proyecto arquitectónico. En 1929, el joven Maharajah de Indore, Yeswant Rao Holkar (1908-1961) educado en Europa, encargó al arquitecto alemán Eckart Muthesius (1904-1989) el diseño de un palacio. El proyecto acabó convirtiéndose en uno de los edificios más representativos de la modernidad europea en cuanto a diseño y tecnología e incluyó algunos trabajos de nombres tan destacados como Le Corbusier, Eileen Grey, Marcel Breuer, Lilly Reich y Constantin Brancusi que planeó un Templo de la Liberación en el que se alojarían algunas de sus esculturas de pájaros, pero que no llegó a realizarse. El palacio contó también con instalaciones de aire acondicionado –no habituales en India– que fueron instaladas por Heinz Riefenstahl, hermano de la famosa cineasta Leni Riefenstahl.

En este entramado de nombres y contextos, realidad y ficción acaban encontrádose y el propio Starling alude al testimonio de Muthesius, el arquitecto, que en cierta forma "ficcionalizó" su implicación en el proyecto, de manera que cuando presentó el trabajo ante un público europeo, retocó las imágenes, escondiendo el tejado que no encajaba con los ideales de la modernidad.

Otro proyecto que habla de viajes es *Red Rivers (In Search of the Elusive Okapi)* (2009), que cuenta la expedición llevada a cabo en el Congo Belga por el zoólogo Herbert Lang. Este viaje, que fue esponsorizado por el Museo de Historia Natural de Nueva York, tenía como motivo la búsqueda del okapi, un mamífero rumiante parecido a una pequeña jirafa. Starling filma un viaje en canoa, que toma como modelos las canoas tradicionales del siglo XIX realizadas en Norteamérica, construidas con dos tipos diferentes de madera (fresno blanco y nogal africano oscuro) para crear las rayas que recuerdan a un okapi. El viaje se inicia en una zona boscosa (que podría emular al Congo) y finaliza en la ciudad de Nueva York. El periplo finaliza en el lugar donde empezó la aventura de Lang, en el Museo de Historia Natural de Nueva York, ante el diorama en el que aparece un okapi. Al igual que Lang hizo miles de fotografías y registró por primera vez la imagen de un okapi, que reveló en una sala de revelado fotográfico que improvisó en una tienda de campaña, Starling filmó las fotografías de su viaje bajo la luz roja de las salas de revelado fotográfico, de manera que da la impresión de que las imágenes han sido seleccionadas a partir de hojas de contactos, han sido ampliadas, reveladas, etc.

La película alude a la historia americana y sus complicadas relaciones con sus vecinos del otro lado del océano, pero también se refiere al poder de la fotografía como herramienta de comunicación y conocimiento. El tono rojizo que remite a la luz de seguridad de las salas de revelado que convierte el río en uno de los ríos rojos del título, recuerda también la tensa relación geopolítica en relación a la colonización.

El consumo y sus paradojas

Otro trabajo que conecta y colapsa geografías y contextos es la instalación *The Long Ton* (2009), formada por dos grandes bloques de mármol que, mediante un sistema de poleas, cuelgan una de otra. La mayor de las piedras, procedente de China tiene un peso de algo más de una tonelada, mientras que la otra piedra, de mármol de Carrara es su réplica exacta, aunque su peso es la cuarta parte. La similitud entre ambas, no lo es en relación a su valor, puesto que pese haber viajado miles de kilómetros, la piedra procedente de China tiene el mismo valor que la pieza procedente de Carrara, aún cuando el peso y tamaño de ésta son significativamente menores.

One Ton II (2005), también llama la atención sobre las contradicciones y los sinsentidos del consumo en nuestro mundo global. Su discurso gira en torno a la cantidad de energía necesaria para producir una pequeña cantidad de platino. Una tonelada de mineral extraído de una mina descubierta de Sudáfrica, lugar que muestran las fotografías de Starling, fue necesario para producir el platino utilizado para revelar a mano las cinco copias fotográficas, platinotipos, que constituyen el trabajo. De nuevo Starling alude a la complejidad de nuestro mundo. El platino, un elemento muy preciado, es necesario por ejemplo para actuar como catalizador en las células de combustibles de hidrógeno, una de las alternativas formas de producción de energía más aconsejables para el futuro y, a la vez, recupera una técnica –el proceso de revelado con platino, muy empleado entre 1860 y 1920– que ha quedado obsoleta.

One Ton II guarda una estrecha relación con *Exposition*, la propuesta que el artista realizó específicamente para el Espai 13 de la Fundació Miró de Barcelona, en el que contrapuso la tecnología contemporánea más avanzada y la evolución del movimiento moderno, tomando como referencia la Exposición Internacional de Barcelona de 1929, un verdadero escaparate tanto de la tecnología como del diseño alemanes de la época, con unos magníficos diseños de exposición creados por Lilly Reich. El punto de partida de *Exposition* fue también un metal precioso, el platino, que en el Espai 13 aparecía doblemente: por una parte, en las fotografías fijadas a la pared –que muestran imágenes del diseño creado por Lilly Reich para la exposición de ingeniería alemana del año 29, obtenidas con el método de impresión fotográfica con platino–; por otra, en la iluminación de dichas fotografías, mediante una célula de combustible de hidrógeno, en cuyo funcionamiento el platino constituye también un elemento esencial, pues actúa como catalizador que hace posible la reacción necesaria entre el hidrógeno y el oxígeno, dando como resultado la producción de corriente eléctrica y una cantidad residual de agua.

En las exposiciones en Málaga y St. Ives, Starling se centra en la historia reciente y las conexiones de ésta con el presente: el pasado fascista de la arquitectura del Centro de Arte Contemporáneo de Málaga; el conflictivo pasado de la Guerra Fría; el pasado expresado a través de obsoletas tecnologías; sobre el pasado de St. Ives como pueblo minero y colonia cultural, y sobre el pasado reciente del artista a través, por ejemplo, de la representación de *Autoxylopyrocycloboros* en una réplica a tamaño real de la galería en la cual se había mostrado previamente.

Ya sea construyendo maquetas a partir de material del propio edificio, inseriendo una arquitectura en otra, magnificando pequeñas partículas, transformando datos en objetos tridimensionales, haciendo visibles procesos tecnológicos, recuperando gestas y viajes, haciendo esfuerzos desproporcionados para los resultados obtenidos o recordando rocambolescas historias, Simon Starling ha desarrollado un pensamiento y un sistema de trabajo configurado a partir de viajes, recorridos, desplazamientos, traducciones, transformaciones, superposiciones, reproducciones, bucles, giros, mezclas de géneros, temporalidades y técnicas, humor, gravedad y poesía. Tal como declaró el jurado que le otorgó el premio Turner en el año 2005, Starling destaca por su *"habilidad única para crear poéticas y unir una gran variedad de narraciones culturales, políticas e históricas"*. Mediante sus deconstrucciones, reconstrucciones y relaciones, Starling no hace sino que evidenciar la complejidad de lo real, el abigarramiento del mundo en el que vivimos y su relación con el pasado más reciente.

Simon Starling
Autoxylopyrocycloboros, 2006

1 En el caso de la Tate, se construyó originariamente en St. Ives para celebrar y representar la colección de obras de la Tate de artistas asociados a la colonia, entre ellos Barbara Hepworth, Naum Gabo, Ben Nicholson, Patrick Heron y Peter Lanyon. En el caso del Pier, alberga la colección de Margaret Gardiner, mecenas y coleccionista que era asidua visitante de St. Ives a mediados del siglo pasado, quien compró muchas de las obras de su colección a artistas que vivían y trabajaban allí.

2 El artista danés Peter Land realizó un vídeo *The Lake* (2000) en el que vestido de cazador se dispone a cazar patos desde una barca. En su primer disparo, agujerea la barca y ésta se hunde lentamente.

3 Lynch, Sean. "Simon Starling and assorted notes on The Atomic Theory", en *Concrete Light*. Limerick City Gallery of Art, Limerck, 2008 (pág. 11).

4 Henry Moore citado en *Art Journal*, Nueva York, primavera 1973 (pág. 286).

Autoxylopyrocycloboros, 2006

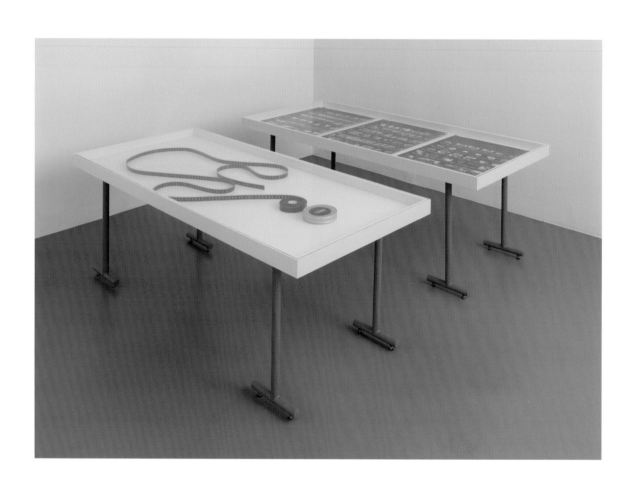

44   **Particle Projection (Loop)**, 2007

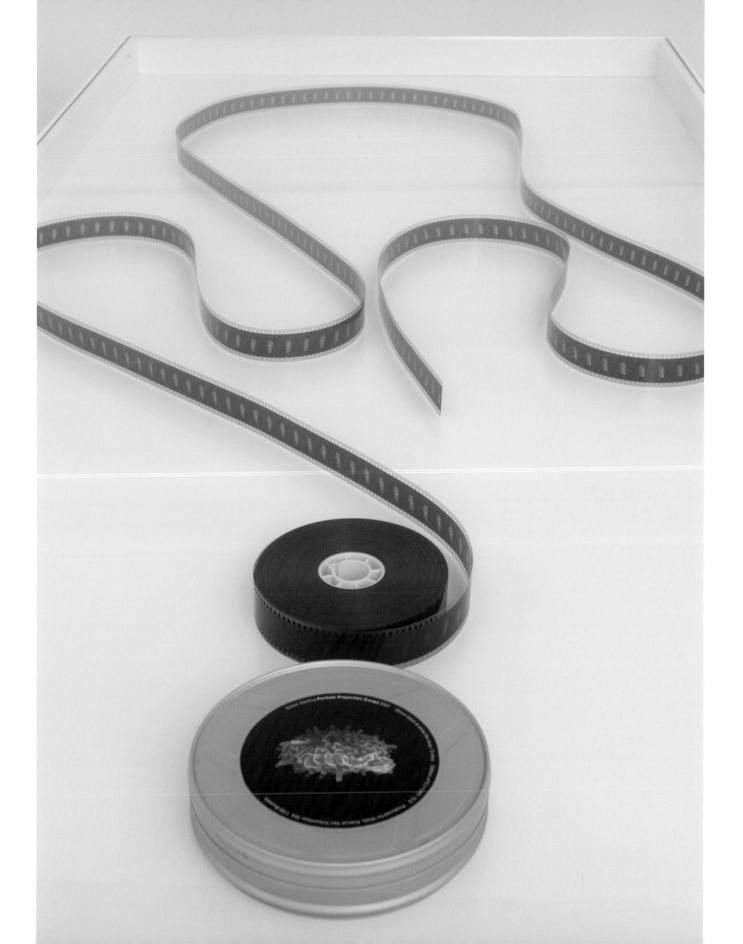

Exposición / Exhibition *Particle Projection (Loop)*, Wiels, Bruselas / Brussels, 2007

Project for a Meeting (Chicago), 2010

Project for a Masquerade (Hiroshima), 2010

Fotogramas de vídeo de producción, estudio Yasuo Miichi, Osaka, 2010 / Production still, studio Yasuo Miichi, Osaka, 2010

300:1 (After Wilhelm Wagenfeld), 2010

300:1 (After Wilhelm Wagenfeld), 2010 (detalle / detail)

Recent history. Concealed narratives

MONTSE BADIA

SIMON STARLING'S work can be described as an intensive quest that involves travel, research and the possibility of making connections between different places, objects and historical and cultural circumstances. Starling's unique and highly distinctive ideas are as humorous as they are erudite and he undertakes specific projects in relation to particular contexts. His trips, the importance of which are equal to or greater than the final destination or end result, reveal hidden relationships, submerged narratives and stories that involve the transformation of one object or substance into another. Starling literally and metaphorically juxtaposes different structures and dynamics. He reveals connections between different times and places. His investigations are, as their very etymology suggests, routes "in pursuit of a mark" or "in search of a clue." In Starling's thinking and in his working procedures one step follows another and each discovery leads on to a new connection. As in a laboratory, the margin of error is part of the process itself. Like a chain reaction, new references or relationships come into being and contribute to establishing new ways of looking, thinking and acting.

At the end of all this research the tale appears. Starling is an investigator, a traveller and also a narrator. The texts and books that accompany his works are an intrinsic part of them, while the data that he brings to light is essential in helping us to come closer to the process and the connections that he establishes. The relationship between narrative and sculpture is constantly renegotiated and explored. Narratives thus accompany works imbued with a powerful presence in the exhibition space. His projects take the form of installations involving elegantly made objects, photographs, films and books. Starling combines and mixes technical strategies in the same way that he plays with the cultural baggage that he brings to bear as a whole on the activity.

Changes of scale

The exhibitions that Simon Starling is presenting at the Contemporary Art Centre of Málaga and Tate St Ives have the same starting point: direct intervention on the architecture of the two institutions with the aim of articulating a group of works that turn around the ideas of change of scale, miniaturisation and magnification, the transfer of digital data into a physical or sculptural form, and, in the reverse direction, the translation of real form into data. The two exhibitions are complementary and in both cases the relationship with the place is modified. The notion of history also plays an important role, referring to recent political and architectural histories in the case of the new work created for Málaga, and to the ancient geological resources that created Cornwall's economic base as a mining region, as well as the town of St Ives' more immediate cultural history as an important international modernist art colony.

At Tate St Ives, Starling begins by confronting two different and geographically remote institutions. In the Tate's building he is creating an exact 1:1 scale reproduction of a gallery space from the Pier Arts Centre in Orkney, Scotland. Both Tate St Ives and the Pier Arts Centre overlook the sea, one at the very Northerly tip of the British Isles and one at the far West, and both have a strong relationship to the 20th century artists colony in St Ives.[1] A couple of years ago Starling showed his slide work *Autoxylopyrocycloboros* (2006) at the Pier Arts Centre. The creation of that work involved sailing on Loch Long in Scotland in a small, "customised" steam boat that was fuelled by the wood of the boat itself until it was finally reduced to a minimum and sunk. On the one hand, the work was inspired by the culture of protest against nuclear submarines, which are frequently to be seen in the waters off this area. On the other, it constitutes a good example of the artist's sense of humour, which is often subtly expressed but which is certainly present in his work and which at times comes close to that of Tom and Jerry cartoons or the Danish artist Peter Land.[2]

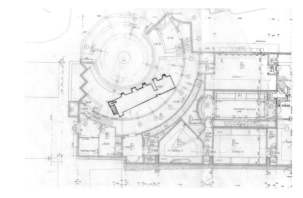

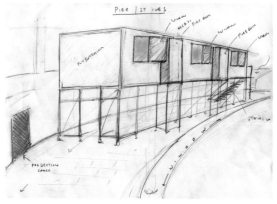

Simon Starling
Reconstrucción del espacio del Pier Art Centre Gallery /
Reconstruction of Pier Art Centre Gallery space

The reconstruction at the Tate of the Orkney gallery creates a spectacular collapsing together of these two disparate spaces, with the replica room appearing – in the curved, glass-fronted gallery space at Tate St Ives – like a kind of ship-in-a-bottle. The work follows on from a number of other architectural sculptures Starling has made over the last few years that often revist an historic narrative or story, but in this case it quite literally re-presents and reinvestigates a piece of his own 'recent history'. *Autoxylopyrocycloboros* is again installed in the space, exactly as it was, accompanied now by one other work, a painting of a steam boat by the St Ives based fisherman and artist Alfred Wallis. Executed in St Ives in around 1934, the painting is now part of the collection of the Pier Arts Centre, returning to St Ives within the 'hull' of the replicated gallery space, set adrift from its usual place. The result is the creation of a number of submerged narratives, of a double-loop type, in which each of the elements and situations appear as related.

The starting point for the principal work in the exhibition in Málaga, *1:1, 1:10, 1:100* (2010), is the reality of the building that houses the Centre, the former Wholesale Market, which is a construction of straight lines and cubic forms that was adapted to the triangular form of the site. The main exhibition gallery emphasises the triangular form of the museums's ground-plan and Starling makes full use of this fact by exhibiting a partial architectural model of the Centre. In addition, and in the same gallery, he shows a model of the museum on a smaller scale. Finally, he proposes building a new one, but this time using materials derived from the construction of the Centre itself and taken from some of its walls. The idea of using the museum's own walls is, as Starling noted in a conversation last October: *"A way of denuding the museum in order to reveal the Fascist-type architecture of the end of the 1930s concealed beneath it. It is no more than a playful way of speaking about the amnesia induced by the new walls and panels that cover the museum's front façade"*.

Starling's new model incorporates the model of the museum, which is not visible and is located "enclosed within the new model" and almost buried in the manner of a mausoleum. Like a set of Russian dolls, the result is the creation of a space that is a hybrid between the model and the building itself, as a result of which the museum houses its own model and, at the same time, generates another one from its own materials in a sort of loop of scales, materials and different functions. As Sean Lynch noted in a text on the exhibition that Simon Starling held in Limerick,[3] Starling's work relates to the ideas of the principal characters in Flann O'Brien's book *The Third Policeman* (1967). The book, with its interest in atomic theory (it focuses, for example, on the atomic theory that proposes the progressive hybridization of the cyclist and the bicycle through material transformation), features a series of somewhat peculiar characters ranging from an eccentric scientist to a man condemned to death, and uses them to discuss the way the world is constructed, deconstructed and reconstructed. One of these characters, a policeman who enjoys craft activities in his spare time, makes a small wooden box that contains another identical one inside it and so on up to twenty-nine boxes, of which only thirteen are visible.

Modifying gestures

Starling's project relating to the CAC Málaga and Tate St Ives buildings has given rise to a group of works that focus on the notion of particles or atoms and which are based on the idea of the transfer of an image's data or codes into physical or sculptural form, or vice versa. One example is *Particle Projection (Loop)* (2007). As in most of Starling's works, the starting point lies in the context. In this case the project was conceived in relation to the inauguration of the Wiels Art Centre in Brussels, which is located in an old distillery. Starling appropriated two references from Belgian culture, which, in characteristic fashion, he ultimately linked up: a famous building from the 1950s and an artist who was a pioneering and fundamental figure for an entire current of subsequent artistic practices based on "institutional criticism." From the starting point of all these references, which he used as his working material, Starling produced a new image of a technology on the point of disappearing.

The references and their interconnections in themselves constituted a story that needs to be explained here. In 1957, the artist Marcel Broodthaers was employed as a labourer on the Atomium building designed by André Waterkeyn for the 1958 Brussels International Fair. The design of the building took the form of a schematic representation of a metal crystal, the abstract symbol of the concept of an atom. Broodthaers recorded the construction of the pavilion in a series of photographs that were subsequently published in the newspaper *Le Patriote Illustré*. When the Atomium was restored, fifty years after it was built, and the deteriorated aluminium was replaced with new triangular panels, a series of black and white photographs was taken that exactly reproduced the one taken by Broodthaers at the time of construction. In a Berlin chemical lab, one of the negatives of the photographs documenting the restoration of the Atomium was stripped of its layer of gel to reveal the silver particles of the developing agent. Seen under an electronic microscope, the fragments of these particles had a spongy, spectral appearance that created a different type of "architecture", filled with labyrinthine structures in constant mutation. One of these particles was then returned to the photographic film, which was considerably enlarged, creating a suggestion of ghostliness.

Particle Projection (Loop) can be presented both as a film projection and as an object in the form of an installation in two display cases, with the 35mm film and the blown-up contacts of the original photographs, expressing this idea of a loop. In this sense, Starling conceives of his works not so much as unique but rather as a constellation of objects, texts, images, books and even talks, which are in some way connected to the main body of the work.

Morphological translations. The case of Henry Moore

Translation is another key concept for Starling. Working close to the global vision of artist Antoni Muntadas' "on translation", Starling transforms or translates one thing into another, from language to codes, from science to technology, from the visible to the invisible, etc. Above all, he is interested in what happens during the process, what changes, what is lost and what appears, and the relationships that are established. Pursuing the idea of data transfer, *Project for a Meeting (Chicago)* (2010) is a new work in which Starling returns to his interest in the art of Henry Moore, one of the most celebrated sculptors of the modern movement. Allusions and references to modern art are habitual in Starling's projects. On the one hand they act as witness to the failure of utopias, and on the other, they express the recovery the nostalgic impulse that underpinned them. *Project for a Meeting (Chicago)* consists of a series of three uranotypes and is part of a body of research on the history of two very similar sculptures by Henry Moore, *Atom Piece* and *Nuclear Energy*, which are located in two strikingly contradictory contexts: the place where the first nuclear reactor was built at the University of Chicago – the starting-place for the so-called Manhattan Project to develop atomic bombs for use in war – and the Hiroshima City Museum of Contemporary Art, the latter located in the city that suffered the terrible consequences of the atomic bomb. The series of three images created by Starling offers a fictitious union between these two works, which are almost identical apart from their size. To close this circle of interconnections, the uranotypes were made using an almost obsolete developing process whose principal constituent is uranium oxide.

The relationship between *Atom Piece* and *Nuclear Energy* is a significant one. *Atom Piece* was a working model for *Nuclear Energy*. Moore himself explained how he devised the project: *"It's a rather strange thing really but I'd already done the idea for this sculpture before Professor McNeill and his colleagues from the University of Chicago came to see me on Sunday morning to tell me about the whole proposition. They told me (which I'd only vaguely known) that Fermi, the Italian nuclear physicist, started or really made the first successful controlled nuclear fission in a temporary building. I think it was a squash court – a wooden building – which from the outside looked entirely unlike where a thing of such an important nature might take place. But this experiment was carried on in secret and it meant that by being successful Man was able to control this huge force for peaceful purposes as well as destructive ones. They came to me to tell me that they thought were such an important event in history took place ought to be marked and they wondered whether I would do a sculpture which would stand on the spot".*[4]

This is not the first time that Starling has been interested in the work and artistic personality of Henry Moore. In *Silver Particle/Bronze (After Henry Moore)* (2008) he took a small black and white photograph taken by Moore himself of his sculpture *Reclining Figure No. 4*. Starling made a circular cut in the photograph, extracting the image of one of the photograph's silver particles. For this project, Starling again used an electron microscope and software designed to build models from multiple images made from different angles. The detail was scanned and manipulated to produce a 3-D model that was translated into the form of a sculpture that was extremely similar to Moore's own. In fact, Moore's working method consisted of making small models that his assistants would enlarge to create his sculptures.

The translation from photography to sculpture using a chain of reproduction refers to the materiality of the work, as Starling sees photography not just in terms of its importance as image, memory base and document but also as a receptacle of metallic particles or, as the artist has noted on various occasions, "as a field of potential sculptures".

Starling's interest in Moore undoubtedly relates to the latter's status as sculptor of the modern age, but also to his own research on artistic institutions. *Project for a Masquerade (Hiroshima)* (2010), is a work that belongs to a three-part exhibition that Starling is currently preparing for The Modern Institute, Glasgow, the Hiroshima City Museum of Contemporary Art, and the Scottish National Gallery of Modern Art, Edinburgh. In it, Starling is undertaking in-depth research into the connection between Moore and the Cold War. *Project for a Masquerade* consists of the presentation of nine characters, subjects of the *Eboshi-ori*, a traditional work of Japanese *Noh* theatre. Six of them are represented by a wooden mask, two of them by bronze masks, and another by a hat. The work tells the story of a young

Simon Starling
Project for a Masquerade (Hiroshima), 2010

nobleman who, with the help of a hat maker, disguises himself in order to escape and start a new life in eastern Japan. In this story of personal reinvention, Starling adds figures associated with Moore within the context of the Cold War in order to look at the double life of *Atom Piece*, which was first made as an independent sculpture but which subsequently acted as the model for *Nuclear Energy* and which had to undergo a change of name, in part because the word "piece" in the title could be confused with "peace", a term far removed from its nuclear context and from the Cold War. The characters in *Project for a Masquerade (Hiroshima)* include Henry Moore, who is the hat maker; Enrico Fermi as the messenger; Joseph Hirshhorn as Kumasaka, an opportunist bandit; James Bond as the gold merchant; Anthony Blunt as the hat maker's wife; and *Atom Piece & Nuclear Energy* as Ushikawa, the young nobleman. The mixture of real and fictitious characters and the fact that the principal role is taken by a sculpture, as well as the female role played by Anthony Blunt, are all indicative of Starling's refined sense of humour. Starling had established connections on earlier occasions between Moore and the Cold War when he analysed his relationship with Anthony Blunt, a double agent who worked for the Soviet NKVD and for the British MI5 service. Blunt was also well known in the art world as a professor of art history at London University, an art critic, champion of Moore's work and director of the Courtauld Institute of Art in London. Through *Project for a Meeting (Chicago)* and *Project for a Masquerade (Hiroshima)* Starling analysed Moore's role as the creator of an homage to the father of nuclear energy, while bearing in mind that he was one of the public sponsors of the Campaign for Nuclear Disarmament. Tightening the loop still further, at that same period Moore sold around fifty sculptures to Joseph Hirshhorn, a businessman and collector who described himself as "Mr Opportunity" and who made his fortune in petrol, gold and uranium prospecting in Canada in the 1960s.

The physical existence of photography

In another recent work, *300:1 (After Wilhelm Wagenfeld)* (2010), Starling returns to his interest in photography as an emotional receptor and also as an element with which to explore its physical existence through the elements that create the images and which are presented in 3-D. The work consists of a series of hand-blown black glass balls, a series of offset prints, and pins for hanging the photographs. The images depict modernist glass objects designed by Bauhaus and inspired by Modernist designers. The size of the glass balls relates to that of the half-tone dots punctured by the pin with which the images on hung on the wall above. Starling's work arose as a consequence of a large installation made

Simon Starling
La Source (demi-teinte), 2009
Exposición / Exhibition *Simon Starling.*
THEREHERETHENTHERE (la Source),
Parc Saint Léger, Centre d'art contemporain de
Pogues-les Eaux, 2009
Foto / Photo: Aurélien Mole

by him in Pouges-les-Eaux, France, in 2009, entitled *La Source (demi-teinte)*. The venue in Pouges-les-Eaux was an old spa where water with health-giving properties was bottled. In this installation Starling presented a light-box that showed a blown-up reproduction of an early 20th-century photograph of the floor of the building where he was now exhibiting, covered with carefully lined up rows of bottles. The workers who carried out the bottling could be seen in the background of the image. Starling made a circular cut in the image. In addition, inside the building he constructed a walkway that ran along one of the narrow corridors, while a series of ramps connected the walkways to the stairs leading to the upper rooms. On the grey concrete floor he arranged 1,036 black glass balls that were hand-made in six different sizes. The effect was that of a huge mesh that produced a distorted vision of the architecture of the building itself. The connection between the black glass balls and the original image was as direct as it was remote: the circle that Starling had cut out of the photograph was blown up to the scale of the building so that each of the dots of the printing was "translated" into its corresponding black glass ball. Seen from the upper balcony, the glass spheres could be read as sections of two of the bottles and a fragment of the floor from the image in the light box.

La Source was an extremely complex project. *300:1 (After Wilhelm Wagenfeld)* is a reduced-scale version of the same project that refers in a more precise manner to the ambiguous space between mass manufacture and bespoke craftsmanship

Stones, evolution and dissemination

In the case of *Archaeopteryx Lithographica* (2008) connections were established between theories of evolution and a type of technology of reproduction that contributed to their dissemination. The work comprises two complementary elements: a sculpture and a group of gelatin silver prints. The sculpture, "Archaeopteryx Lithographica" takes its name from one of the most important fossils ever found. Through this work Starling explores a key moment in the 19th century when the growth of offset printing had a major influence on the dissemination of theories of evolution which, through this newly discovered fossil, had been able to establish a relationship between dinosaurs and birds.

Archaeopteryx thus became a lithographic series consisting of six lithographs that link the various realities of the image: a lithographic reproduction of the text photographs, the photograph of the lithograph of the fossils on the lithographic stone, the lithographic impression of the photograph of the fossils, etc.

Journeys through history and technique

D1-Z1 (22,686,575:1) made in 2009 should be singled out with regard to the above-mentioned idea of transferring data from one medium to another and even from one dimension to another. The work refers to what was considered to be the world's first programmable computer, the Z1. It was designed in 1936 by the engineer and artist Konrad Zuse (1910-1995) and occupied an entire room. With 172 bytes of memory and the ability to add, subtract, multiply and divide, the Z1 was privately financed and literally home-made in Zuse's parents' apartment in Berlin. Completed in 1938, it was "programmed" from a punched tape feed into a reader. Zuse punched his programmes on 35mm photographic film.

D1-Z1 is a 30-second long sequence showing an image of the machine itself in action. As is sometimes the case with Starling, the laborious effort involved in his working methods seems out of proportion to the results, while on other occasions these methods seem to come close to a critique of the pressure to achieve dramatic effects and to save time characteristic of the present day. The images in *D1-Z1 (222,686,575:1)* are thus generated using animation technology

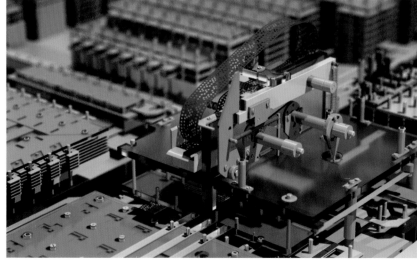

Simon Starling
D1-Z1 (22,686,575:1), 2009
(Fotograma / Still)

including surface-rendering programmes produced in Berlin. Creating this simple, 30 second animated sequence, which depicts the punched film reader (a small part of the huge machine) required 3,992,837,240 bytes of information, in other words, more than 22 million times the memory of Z1. This virtual, computer-generated reconstruction was then transferred onto 35mm film and was shown on another celebrated piece of mid-century technology, a Dresden D1 projector, which had been adapted for loop projection. The projected image, which is slightly blurred, shows the machine itself in action, with the film moving through it. As hypnotic as it is formalist, the work is nothing less than an homage to Zuse's perseverance, which is close to Starling's own. It also involves a humorous approach to a way of doing things which is far remote from present day practices. In fact, all the machines and techniques brought together in these projects, from Zuse's computer to film developing with uranium or the use of artisan, hand blown glass in the modern day are used by Starling as elements in a reflection on a contemporary reality that seems to us far more de-materialised.

Using this approach, Starling creates a journey between two different contexts: historical and technical. He combines high technology with low technology to produce an image of the first prototype of a programmable calculator. Starling's interest in the image starts from the relationship that it could establish with the machine that reproduces it, with a desire to show the mechanism, what it represents and its historical and social connotations.

Like another, earlier work, *Wilhelm Noak oHG* (2006), in which a 35mm film projects the construction of a staircase while the actual film gradually rolls itself around this same staircase, *D1-Z1 (22,686,575:1)* documents its own method of creation. In both cases we reencounter the loop in relation to the history of the technique and the support of the film, both of which take on contemporary meaning in a space filled with new implications.

Six degrees of separation

Starling's working procedure, in which he gradually establishes a chain of connections that might seem theoretically inconceivable, connects to the theory that was proposed in the short story *Chains* (1929) by the Hungarian writer Frigyes Karinthy and popularised in a play by John Guare. Karinthy maintained that anyone in the world could be connected to anyone else through a chain of acquaintances that involves no more than five intermediaries. The six degrees of separation with which Starling works not only connect people but also facts, situations and discoveries.

Three Birds, Seven Stories, Interpolations and Bifurcations (2008) recounts the story of a European architect from whom an Indian maharajah commissioned an ambitious architectural project. In 1929 the young, European educated Maharajah of Indore, Yeshwant Rao Holkar (1908-1961), commissioned the German architect Eckart Muthesius (1904-1989) to design him a palace. The project ultimately become one of the most famous buildings of European Modernism with regard to design and technology and involved the work of leading names such as Le Corbusier, Eileen Grey, Marcel Breuer, Lilly Reich and Constantin Brancusi. The latter designed a Temple of Liberation to house some of his sculptures of birds, but this was never made. The palace also had air conditioning (unusual in India) installed by Heinz Riefenstahl, brother of the famous filmmaker Leni Riefenstahl.

Reality and fiction combine in this tapestry of names and contexts and Starling makes reference to the account offered by Muthesius himself, who to some extent "fictionalised" his involvement in the project: when he presented it to a European public he retouched the images, concealing the roof that did not conform to Modernist precepts.

Another project involving journeys is *Red Rivers (In Search of the Elusive Okapi)* (2009) which offers an account of the expedition undertaken by the zoologist Herbert Lang in

Simon Starling
Red Rivers (In Search of the Elusive Okapi), 2009
Foto / Photo: Cary Whittier, Kasper Akhøj, Simon Starling

the Belgian Congo. The purpose of the trip, which was sponsored by the Natural History Museum in New York, was to look for the okapi, a ruminant similar to a small giraffe. Starling films a canoe trip, taking as his model one of the traditional 19th-century canoes made in North America, which was built from two different kind of wood, white ash and dark African walnut, to create stripes which suggest an okapi's marking. The journey starts in a wooded area (that could almost be the Congo) and ends in the city of New York, presenting a slow transition in which culture takes over from nature. It concludes in the place where Lang's adventure started, in the Natural History Museum of New York, in front of the diorama in which an okapi is to be seen. Just as Lang took thousands of photographs and recorded the okapi for the first time, developing his prints in an improvised lab in a tent, Starling filmed the photographs of his trip under the red light used in developing rooms. The result is to give the impression that the images have been selected from contact sheets, blown up, and developed, etc.

The film refers to American history and its complex relationship with Europe, as well as to the power of photography as a tool of communication and knowledge. The reddish tone that brings to mind the safety light in developing rooms and which turns the river into one of the "red rivers" of the title, also recalls geo-political tensions in the context of colonialism.

Consumption and its paradoxes

Another work that connects to and dismantles locations and contexts is the installation *The Long Ton* (2009). It consists of two large blocks of marble, one of which is suspended from the other through a system of pulleys. The larger of the two comes from China and weighs over a tonne, while the other block, which is made of Carrara marble, is an exact replica although it weighs only a quarter of the Chinese one. Their similarity does not extend to their value, as despite having travelled thousands of kilometres, the Chinese block is worth the same as the one from Carrara, even though the Italian one is significantly lighter and smaller.

One Ton II (2005) also draws attention to the contradictions and nonsensical elements within modern-day global consumption. The concept of this work focuses on the amount of energy needed to produce a small amount of platinum. A tonne of the mineral extracted from an open-cast mine in South Africa, shown in Starling's photographs, was needed to produce the platinum used to hand develop the five platinotype prints that make up this work. Once again Starling refers to the complexity of the modern world. Among the uses of platinum, which is a highly prized precious metal, is that of catalyser in hydrogen fuel cells, which are one of the most promising sources of alternative energy of the future. In addition, platinum is used in the platinotype method of photographic development, widely employed between 1860 and 1920 but now obsolete.

One Ton II is closely related to Exposition, the work made by Starling for the Espai 13 of the Fundació Miró in Barcelona. Here, the artist juxtaposed cutting-edge contemporary technology and the evolution of the modern movement, taking as his starting point the 1929 Barcelona International Exhibition, an event that was a showcase for both German technology and design of the period, with magnificent displays designed by Lilly Reich. Another key element in Exposition was once again platinum, which has a double role in this work; firstly in the photographs on the wall that show some of the designs by Lilly Reich for the display on German engineering at the 1929 Exhibition, and which were printed using the platinotype technique; and on the other, in the way these photographs are lit, using a hydrogen fuel cell, in which platinum is a key element as it acts as a catalyser that enables the necessary reaction between hydrogen and oxygen to come about, resulting in the production of electric current and a residual amount of water.

In the exhibitions in Malaga and St Ives, Simon Starling has focused on recent history and its connections with the present; on

Simon Starling
The Long Ton, 2009 (detalle / detail)
Foto / Photo: Jens Ziehe

the Fascist past of the architecture of the Contemporary Art Centre of Málaga; on the conflictive past of the Cold War; on the past expressed through obsolete technologies; on St Ives' past as a mining town and a cultural colony; and on the artist's own recent past through, for example, the re-presentation of *Autoxylopyrocycloboros* in a full size replica of the gallery in which it was previously shown.

Whether constructing architectural models using material from the building itself, inserting one building inside another, magnifying small particles, transforming data into 3-D objects, making technological processes visible, rediscovering epic undertakings and journeys, making efforts out of all proportion to the results obtained or recalling bizarre stories, Simon Starling has evolved a conceptual approach and a working method based on journeys, routes, geographical shifts, translations, transformations, superimpositions, reproductions, loops and turns, and which mix genres, time-frames, techniques, humour, gravity and poetry. As the jury that awarded him the 2005 Turner Prize noted, Starling is outstanding for his: "[...] unique ability to create poetic narratives that draw together a wide variety of cultural, political and historical references." Through his deconstructions, reconstructions and connections, Starling reveals the complexity of the real, the jumbled, crowded nature of the world in which we exist and its relationship to the most recent past.

---

1 In the case of the Tate, it was originally built in St Ives to celebrate and represent the Tate's collection of works by artists associated with the colony, including Barbara Hepworth, Naum Gabo, Ben Nicholson, Patrick Heron and Peter Lanyon. In the case of the Pier, it houses the collection of Margaret Gardiner, a patron and collector who was a frequent visitor to St Ives through the middle of the last century, and who bought many of the works in her collection from the artists living and working there.

2 The Danish artist Peter Land made a video entitled *The Lake* (2000) in which he dressed as a hunter and presented himself about to shoot duck from a boat. His first shot made a hole in the boat, which slowly sunk.

3 Lynch, Sean, "Simon Starling and assorted notes on The Atomic Theory", in *Concrete Light*, Limerick City Gallery of Art, Limerick, 2008, p. 11

4 Henry Moore quoted in *Art Journal*, New York, Spring 19, p. 286.

Archaeopteryx Lithographica, 2008

Lithograph print of the feather impression preserved in a slab of Solnhofen Lithographic Limestone of Bavaria and reported by HERMANN VON MEYER (1861a). This illustration appeared in VON MEYER's article of 1862.

D1 - Z1 (22,686,575:1), 2009

Red Rivers (In Search of the Elusive Okapi), 2009

One Ton II, 2005

The Long Ton, 2009

88   **Inventar-Nr.8573 (Man Ray) 4m-400 nm**, 2006

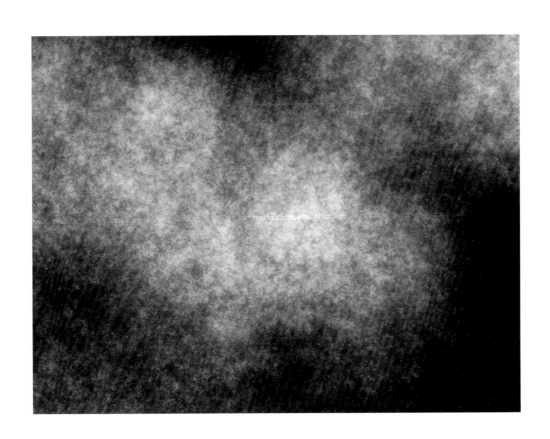

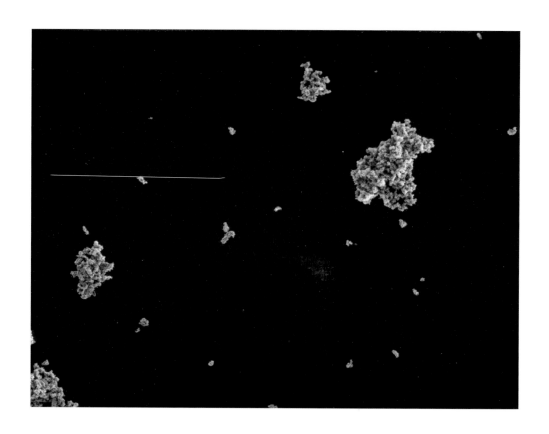

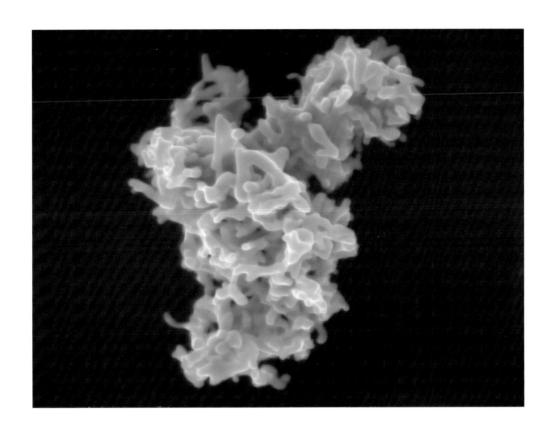

Vistas de la exposición / Installation views *Simon Starling. Recent History*, CAC Málaga, 2010

Lista de obras | List of Works

1:1, 1:10; 1:100, 2010 M
Placas de pladur y DM recicladas, maqueta del CAC Málaga a escala 1:100 /
Recycled plasterboard and MDF, 1:100 architecture model of CAC Málaga
207 x 1.110 x 543 cm

Archaeopteryx Litographica, 2008-2009 T
Piedra caliza de Solnhofen y tinta / Solnhofen lithographica limestone, ink
Piedra / Limestone: 53 x 43 x 7 cm. Peana / Plinth 110 x 66 x 55 cm
Colección / Collection Lang, Austria

Autoxylopyrocycloboros, 2006 T
Proyector de diapositivas Gotschmann. Diapositivas color 38,6 x 7 cm /
Gotschmann slide projector. Colour transparencies 38,6 x 7 cm
Dimensiones variables / Variable dimensions

Particle Projection (Loop), 2007 M
[Proyección de partículas (Bucle)]
Película b/n de 35 mm, 6 contactos en gelatina de plata ampliados, 2 vitrinas /
35mm black & white film, 6 enlarged gelatin silver contact prints, 2 vitrines
2 vitrinas de / 2 vitrines of 82,5 x 100 x 225 cm c/u / each
Cortesía el artista y la Galleria Franco Noero, Turín /
Courtesy the artist and Galleria Franco Noero, Turin

Project for a Meeting (Chicago), 2010 M
[Proyecto para un encuentro (Chicago)]
3 uranotipos / 3 uranotype photographic prints
50,8 x 40,6 cm c/u / each
Cortesía el artista y neugerriemschneider, Berlín /
Courtesy the artist and neugerriemschneider, Berlin

Project for a Masquerade (Hiroshima), 2010 T
[Proyecto para una mascarada (*Hiroshima*)]
2 de 9 máscaras / 2 of 9 masks:
The Hat Maker/Henry Moore
Máscara de madera tallada con soporte de metal / Carved wooden mask with metal stand
Ushiwaka/Atom Piece
Máscara de bronce con soporte de metal / Cast bronze mask with metal stand
Cortesía el artista y The Modern Institute, Glasgow /
Courtesy the artist and The Modern Institute, Glasgow

300:1 (After Wilhelm Wagenfeld), 2010 M T
[300:1 (Después de Wilhelm Wagenfeld)]
Bolas de vidrio soplado a mano, impresiones *offset* en blanco y negro y alfileres /
Hand blown glass balls, black & white offset prints and pins
Dimensiones variables / Variable dimensions
Cortesía el artista y neugerriemschneider, Berlín /
Courtesy the artist and neugerriemschneider, Berlin

Archaeopteryx Lithographica, 2008 M T
6 litografías / 6 lithographic prints
56 x 76 cm c/u / each
Cortesía el artista y neugerriemschneider, Berlín /
Courtesy the artist and neugerriemschneider, Berlin

Red Rivers (In Search of the Elusive Okapi), 2009 T
[Red Rivers (En busca del escurridizo okapi)]
Vídeo HD, proyector HD, reproductor multimedia, altavoces /
HD Video, HD projector, media player, speakers
24' 12"
Cortesía el artista y Casey Kaplan, Nueva York /
Courtesy the artist and Casey Kaplan, Nueva York

D1 - Z1 (22,686,575:1), 2009 M T
Proyector Dresde D1, máquina de *loop*, amplificador, altavoces,
película de 35 mm con sonido en *loop* /
Dresden D1 Film Projector, loop machine, amplifier,
speakers, 35 mm black and white film loop with sound
30 segundos / 30 seconds
Dimensiones variables / Dimensions variable
Cortesía el artista y neugerriemschneider, Berlín /
Courtesy the artist and neugerriemschneider, Berlin

One Ton II, 2005 M T
[Una tonelada II]
5 platinotipos hechos a mano en marcos acrílicos /
5 handmade platinum/palladium prints in acrylic boxes
75,5 x 94,5 x 6 cm c/u / each
Cortesía el artista y neugerriemschneider, Berlín /
Courtesy the artist and neugerriemschneider, Berlin

Inventar-Nr.8573 (Man Ray) 4m-400 nm, 2006 T
[Inventario Nº 8573 (Man Ray) 4m-400nm]
Proyección de diapositivas 8 min.
80 diapositivas b/n tamaño medio, 2 proyectores de diapositivas de tamaño medio,
unidad de disco Kodak S- AV
80 transparencias b/n de 6 x 7 cm c/u, 2 proyectores de diapositivas Gotschmann,
Kodak PDC dissolve control unit, reproductor de CD /
Slide projection 8 min.
80 medium format black & white slides, 2 medium format slide projectors,
Kodak S- AV Unit CD
80 black & white transparencies 6 x 7cm each 2 x Gotschmann slide projectors,
Kodak PDC dissolve control unit CD, and CD player
Dimensiones variables / Variable dimensions
Cortesía el artista y neugerriemschneider, Berlín /
Courtesy the artist and neugerriemschneider, Berlin

The Long Ton, 2009 T
[Tonelada larga]
1 bloque de mármol chino, 1 bloque de mármol de Carrara, sistema de poleas,
abrazaderas, grilletes de cuerda /
Chinese marble block, 1 Carrara marble block, pulley system, clamps, rope shackles
Bloque de mármol chino / Chinese marble block: 90 x 120 x 50 cm
Bloque de mármol de Carrara / Carrara marble block: 59 x 74 x 31 cm
Dimensiones variables / Variable dimensions
Cortesía el artista y neugerriemschneider, Berlín /
Courtesy the artist and neugerriemschneider, Berlin

Pier (for Autoxylopyrocycloboros, 2006 and St Ives Harbour and Godrevy, circa 1934-1938), 2010 T
[Muelle *(para Autoxylopyrocycloboros, 2006 y St Ives Harbour and Godrevy, circa 1934-1938)*]
Técnica mixta, 38 transparencias de tamaño medio (6 x 7 cm), 1 proyector de diapositivas
Gotschmann G8585 AV 67, óleo y lápiz sobre cartulina /
Mixed media, 38 x medium format color transparencies (6 x 7cm), 1 Gotschmann G8585 AV 67
slide projector, oil and pencil on card
60 x 380 x 1220 cm
Cortesía el artista y The Modern Institute, Glasgow /
Courtesy the artist and The Modern Institute, Glasgow

China Clay Stack, 2011 T
[Montón de arcilla china]
Impresión offset sobre papel revestido de caolín / Offset print on kaolin-rich coated paper
80 x 52 cm
Cortesía el artista y The Modern Institute, Glasgow /
Courtesy the artist and The Modern Institute, Glasgow

Undercroft/Inversion, 2011 T
[Vacío / Inversión]
Negativo blanco y negro / Black and white negative
12 x 10 cm / 5 x 4 large format transparency
Cortesía el artista y The Modern Institute, Glasgow /
Courtesy the artist and The Modern Institute, Glasgow

CAC Málaga: M
TATE St Ives: T

Ultrasuperleggera, 2003
Fibra de carbón / Carbon Fibre
45 x 41 x 83 cm

Simon Starling

Epsom, Reino Unido / United Kingdom, 1967
Vive y trabaja en Copenhague /
Lives and works in Copenhagen

EXPOSICIONES INDIVIDUALES / SOLO EXHIBITIONS

2010
Recent History, CAC Málaga, Centro de Arte
Contemporáneo de Málaga, España; Tate St Ives,
Reino Unido (cat.)
Never The Same River (Possible Futures, Probable Past),
Camden Art Centre, Londres
Project for a Masquerade (Hiroshima): The Mirror Room,
The Modern Institute, Glasgow (cat.)

2009
Red White Blue, Casey Kaplan, Nueva York, EE. UU.
Thereherethenthere (Oeuvres 1997-2009), MAC/VAL,
Vitry sur Seine, Francia
Thereherethenthere (la Source), Parc Saint Leger, Centre
d'art contemporain, Pougues- les-Eaux, Francia
Poul Henningsen - BLACK OUT (with Superflex),
Kunsthallen Brandts, Odense, Dinamarca
Simon Starling, Temporäre Kunsthalle Berlin, Berlín,
Alemania
The Long Ton, neugerriemschneider, Berlín, Alemania

2008
The Nanjing Particles, MassMOCA, North Adams, EE. UU.
Concrete Light, Limerick City Gallery of Art, Limerick,
Irlanda
Plant Room, Kunstraum Dornbirn, Dornbirn, Austria (cat.)
Project for a Public Sculpture (After Thomas Annan),
The Modern Institute, Glasgow, Reino Unido
*Three Birds, Seven Stories, Interpolation and
Bifurcations*, Galleria Franco Noero, Turín, Italia
Ludwig Muzeum - Museum of Contemporary Art,
Budapest, Hungría
Cuttings (supplements), The Powerplant, Toronto,
Canadá (cat.)

2007
Immagini, Forme e Natura delle Alpi, Fondazione Gruppo
Credito Valtellinese, Sondrio, Italia
Simon Starling - Kintsugi, Appenzell Biennale,
Schaukasten, Herisau, Suiza
Simon Starling - Nachbau, Museum Folkwang, Essen,
Alemania (cat.)
László Moholy-Nagy & Simon Starling, Presentation House
Gallery, Vancouver, Canadá
Particle Projection (Loop), Wiels, Bruselas, Bélgica
Casey Kaplan, Nueva York, EE. UU.

2006
Heidelberger Kunstverein, Heidelberg, Alemania
Wilhelm Noack oHG, neugerriemschneider, Berlín,
Alemania
24 hr. Tangenziale, Galleria Franco Noero, Turín,
Italia (cat.)

2005
C.A.M., Void, Derry, Irlanda
Cuttings, Museum für Gegenwartskunst, Basilea, Suiza

2004
Tabernas Desert Run, The Modern Institute, Glasgow,
Reino Unido
Exposition, Fundació Joan Miró, Barcelona, España
One Ton, neugerriemschneider, Berlín, Alemania
Casey Kaplan, Nueva York, EE. UU.

2003
Museo d'Arte Contemporanea, Roma, Italia (cat.)
Djungel, South London Gallery, Londres, Reino Unido
Carbon, Städtische Ausstellungshalle am Hawerkamp
Münster, Alemania (cat.)
Villa Arson, Niza, Francia

2002
Museum of Contemporary Art (con Mathew Jones),
Sídney, Australia (cat.)
Ucla Hammer Museum, Los Ángeles, EE. UU.
Kakteenhaus, Portikus, Fráncfort, Alemania (cat.)

Djungel, Dundee Contemporary Arts, Dundee, Reino
Unido (cat.)
FLAGA (1972-2000), Galleria Franco Noero, Turín,
Italia (cat.)
Inverted Retrograde Theme, Casey Kaplan, Nueva York,
EE. UU.

2001

Simon Starling and Poul Henningsen, Cooper Gallery,
University of Dundee, Dundee, Reino Unido (cat.)
Burn-Time / Reading Room, Galerie für Gegenwartskunst,
Barbara Claassen-Schmal, Bremen, Alemania
Burn-Time, neugerriemschneider, Berlín, Alemania
Burn-Time, Lichthaus plus neue Kunst, Bremen,
Alemania (cat.)
Work, made ready, Les Baux de Provence; Kunstverein
Hamburg, Hamburgo, Alemania
CMYK / RGB, Frac Languedoc-Roussillon, Montpellier,
Francia (cat.)
Inverted Retrograde Theme, Rescued Rhododendron,
Secession, Viena, Austria (cat.)
John Hansard Gallery, University of Southhampton,
Reino Unido (cat.)

2000

Studio 2000, Colonia, Alemania
Metod 1: Simon Starling, Signal, Malmö, Suecia
Camden Arts Center, Londres, Reino Unido (cat.)
Fundacão Serralves, Oporto, Portugal
Preston Museum and Art Gallery, Preston, Reino Unido

1999

Signal, Malmö, Suecia
Blinky Palermo Prize, Galerie für Zeitgenössiche Kunst,
Leipzig, Alemania (cat.)

1998

Moderna Museet Project Room, Estocolmo, Suecia (cat.)

1997

Blue Boat Black, Transmission Gallery, Glasgow,
Reino Unido (cat.)

1995

An Eichbaum Pils beer can... , The Showroom, Londres,
Reino Unido (cat.)

EXPOSICIONES COLECTIVAS / GROUP EXHIBITIONS

2010

Unsichtbare Schatten - Bilder der Verunsicherung, MARTa
Herford, Herford, Alemania
Les Lendemains d'hier, Musée d'art contemporain de
Montréal, Montreal, Canadá (cat.)
lost and found, neugerriemschneider, Berlín, Alemania
FALL OUT - art, desire and disengagement, Gl Holtegaard,
Holte, Dinamarca

2009

Making Worlds // Fare Mundi, 53rd International Art
Exhibition. La Biennale di Venezia, Venecia, Italia
Altermodern, Tate Triennial, Tate Britain, Londres,
Reino Unido
The Quick and the Dead, Walker Art Center, Mineápolis,
EE. UU.

2008

Reality Check, Statens Museum for Kunst, Copenhague,
Dinamarca
Close up, Fruitmarket Gallery, Edimburgo, Reino Unido
Scotland and Venice, Pier Arts Centre, Orkney,
Reino Unido
Master Humphrey's Clock, De Appel, Ámsterdam,
Países Bajos
ITALIA ITALIE ITALIEN ITALY WLOCHY, ARCOS, Museo
d'Arte Contemporanea Sannio, Benevento, Italia
P2P, Casino Luxembourg - Forum d'art contemporain,
Luxemburgo
Of this tale, I cannot guarantee a single word, Royal
College of Art, Londres, Reino Unido (cat.)
Greenwashing, Fondazione Sandretto Re Rebaudengo,
Turín, Italia
*The Greenroom: Reconsidering the Documentary and
Contemporary Art*, Center for Curatorial Studies, Bard
College, Annandale-on-Hudson, EE. UU.

2007

Wenn Handlungen Form werden. Ein neuer Realismus in der Kunst seit den fünfziger Jahren, Neues Museum, Núremberg, Alemania
Turner Prize: A Retrospective, Tate Britain, Londres, Reino Unido
This Winter, Casey Kaplan, Nueva York, EE. UU.
Hiram, Galleria Antonio Ferrara, Reggio Emilia, Italia
Nachvollziehungsangebote, Kunsthalle Exnergasse, Viena, Austria
Biennale d'art contemporain de Lyon, Francia
Out of art, dalla collezione di Ernesto Esposito, Centre PasquArt, Biel, Suiza
Des mondes perdus, CAPC, musée d'art contemporain de Bordeaux, Burdeos, Francia
Made in Germany, kestnergesellschaft, Hannover, Alemania (cat.)
Held together with water, Kunst aus der Sammlung Verbund, MAK-Ausstellungshalle, Viena, Austria (cat.)
entreprises singulières, MAC/VAL Musée d'art contemporain du Val-de-Marne, Vitry-sur Seine, Francia
Sharjah Biennale, Sharjah, Emiratos Árabes Unidos
Moscow Biennale of Contemporary Art, Moscú, Rusia (cat.)

2006

Casa aberta, INHOTIM centro de arte contemporãnea, Minas Gerais, Brasil
Ecotopia, The Second ICP Trienal of Photography and Video, International Center of Photography, Nueva York, EE. UU.
Busan Biennale, Busan, Corea
Home for lost ideas, Schönhauser Allee 167c, Berlín, Alemania
Periferic 7: Focussing Iasi, International Biennial for Contemporary Art, Ia i, Rumanía
Verkehrskultur, Westfälischer Kunstverein, Münster, Alemania (cat.)
Objet à part, La Galerie, Noisy-le-Sec, Francia
Strange I've seen that face before, Städtisches Museum Abteiberg, Mönchengladbach, Alemania
If I didn't exist you'd have to invent it: a partial Showroom history, The showroom, Londres, Reino Unido

2005

36 x 27 x 10, White Cube Berlin im ehemaligen Palast der Republik, Berlín, Alemania
Drive. Cars in Contemporary Art, Galleria D'Arte Moderna, Bolonia, Italia
Lichtkunst aus Kunstlicht, ZKM, Museum für Neue Kunst, Karlsruhe, Alemania
The Party, Casey Kaplan, Nueva York, EE. UU.
Mouvement Des Deux Côtés Du Rhin, Museum Ludwig, Colonia, Alemania
Omaggio al Quadrato, Galleria Franco Noero, Turín, Italia
Ambiance Des Deux Côtés Du Rhin, K21 Kunstsammlung NRW, Düsseldorf, Alemania
Turner Prize 2005, Tate Britain, Londres, Reino Unido
Mouvement des deux côtés du Rhin, Museum Ludwig, Colonia, Alemania
paralleles leben, Frankfurter Kunstverein, Fráncfort, Alemania (cat.)
The Failure, Korridor, Berlín, Alemania
Universal Experience: Art, Life and the Tourist's Eye, The Museum of Contemporary Art Chicago, EE. UU. (cat.)
Goodbye, Fourteenth Street, Casey Kaplan, Nueva York, EE. UU.

2004

Bienal de São Paulo, São Paulo, Brasil
Schöner Wohnen, kunst van heden voor alle dagen, BE-PART, Platform voor actuele kunst, Waregem, Bélgica (cat.)
In the beginning there was the journey, 28. Bienal de Arte de Pontevedra, España (cat.)
LAB, Kröller Müller Museum Park, Otterlo, Países Bajos

2003

Outlook, "The Factory", Athens school of Fine Arts, Atenas, Grecia (cat.)
Galleria Franco Noero, Turín, Italia
Hands up, baby, hands up, Oldenburger Kunstverein, Oldenburg, Alemania
Zenomap. New works from Scotland for the Venice Biennale, 50. Biennale di Venezia, Venecia, Italia
Global Navigation System, Palais de Tokyo, París, Francia (cat.)

I Moderni. The Moderns, Castello di Rivoli, Turín, Italia (cat.)
Skulptur-Biennale, Münsterland, Alemania (cat.)
Interplay, The Moore Building, Miami, EE. UU. (cat.)

2002

lapdissolve; Casey Kaplan, Nueva York, EE. UU.
Barby Asante, Journey into the East, The showroom, Londres, Reino Unido
Zusammenhänge herstellen, Kunstverein in Hamburg, Hamburgo, Alemania (cat.)
Der globale Komplex - continental drift, Grazer Kunstverein, Graz, Austria
No return, Positionen aus der Sammlung Haubrok; Museum Abteiberg, Mönchengladbach, Alemania
Exchange & Transform, Kunstverein München, Múnich, Alemania

2001

Der Larsen Effekt- Prozesshafte Resonanzen in der zeitgenössischen Kunst, Centrum für Gegenwartskunst Linz, Austria; Casino Luxembourg, Luxemburgo
Squatters #2, Witte de With, Center for Contemporary Art, Róterdam, Países Bajos
Here + Now, Scottish Art 1990-2001, Dundee Contemporary Arts, Dundee, Reino Unido
Total object complete with missing parts; Tramway, Glasgow, Reino Unido
Silk Purse, Arnolfini, Bristol, Reino Unido
Strategies against architecture II, Laboratorio per l'arte contemporanea, Pisa, Italia
Dévoler vivent les Frac, L'institut d' art contemporain, Villeurbanne, Francia
Squatters, Museu Serralves, Oporto, Portugal
7 New Artists' Commissions for the Park to be completed by early 2002, National Park, Scotland, Loch Lomond, Reino Unido; Casey Kaplan, Nueva York, EE. UU.
circles °4, Zentrum für Kunst und Medientechnologie, Karlsruhe, Alemania
Experiment the Real, Albi, Francia
Open Country, Le Musée cantonal des Beaux-Arts, Lausana, Suiza (cat.)

2000

robières /roberies, Marres-Centre for Contemporary Art, Maastricht, Países Bajos
play-use, Witte de With, Center for Contemporary Art, Róterdam, Países Bajos
futureperfect, Centre for Visual Arts, Cardiff, Reino Unido
Manifesta 3. European Biennal of Contemporary Art, Liubliana, Eslovenia (cat.)
Artifice, Deste Foundation - Centre for Contemporary Art, Atenas, Grecia
Grant Selwyn Fine Arts, Beverly Hills, EE. UU.
What If /Tänk om, Moderna Museet, Estocolmo, Suecia (cat.)
The British Art Show, itinerante (cat.)
If I Ruled the World, CCA, Glasgow, Reino Unido
Spacecraft, Bluecoat, Liverpool, Reino Unido (cat.)
Micropolitiques, Le Magasin, Grenoble, Francia (cat.)
The work in this space is a response to the existing conditions and /or work previously shown within the space, neugerriemscheider, Berlín, Alemania (cat.)

1999

The Office of Misplaced Events, 51 Cleveland St, Londres, Reino Unido
Fireworks, De Appel, Ámsterdam, Países Bajos
Fang den Hut, Galerie Eigen & Art, Leipzig, Alemania
Artist's Projects, Dundee Contemporary Arts, Dundee, Reino Unido
Tyrebagger Sculpture Project, Aberdeenshire, Reino Unido
The Living Art Museum, Reikiavik, Islandia
Un Certain, ATA Centre d''Art Contemporain, Sofía, Bulgaria
Dummy, Catalyst Arts Project, Belfast, Irlanda
Thinking Aloud, Camden Arts Centre, Londres, Reino Unido

1998

Family, Inverlith House, Edimburgo, Reino Unido
Strolling, Museum of Modern Art at Heide, Melbourne, Australia (cat.)
Reconstructions, Smart project Space, Ámsterdam, Países Bajos (cat.)
Bad Faith, Three Month Gallery, Liverpool, Reino Unido (cat.)
Bad Faith, Waygood Gallery, Newcastle, Reino Unido
Lost and Found, Decima Gallery, Londres, Reino Unido

The Modern Institute at Sadie Coles HQ, Londres,
Reino Unido

1997
L'Automne dans toutes ses collections, MAC, Marsella,
Francia
Nerve, Artspace, Sídney, Australia (cat.)
Glasgow, Kunsthalle Bern, Berna, Suiza (cat.)
B.c.c, Cleveland and The Tannery, Londres, Reino Unido
Fishing for Shapes, Künstlerhaus Bethanien, Berlín,
Alemania
Wish You Were Here Too, Hill St., Glasgow, Reino Unido

1996
After you made me soft again, Galerie Barz, Hannover,
Alemania (cat.)
Once Removed, Laure Genillard, Londres, Reino Unido
Kilt ou Double, La Vigie, Nîmes, Francia
Sick Building, Transmission Gallery, Copenhague,
Dinamarca
City Limits, Staffordshire University, Stoke on Trent, Reino
Unido (cat.)
Fishing for Shapes, Projektraum Voltmerstrasse,
Hannover, Alemania

1995
Maikäfer Flieg, Bunker Köln-Ehrenfeld, Colonia,
Alemania (cat.)
Kabinett für Zeichnung, Kampnagel, Hamburgo, Alemania
About Place, Collective Gallery, Edimburgo, Reino Unido

1994
Institute of Cultural Anxiety, ICA, Londres, Reino Unido (cat.)
Miniatures, The Agency, Londres, Reino Unido
Oriel Mostyn Open, Oriel Mostyn, Llandudno, Sudáfrica
Modern Art, Transmission Gallery, Glasgow, Reino Unido
*Die Zweite Wirklichkeit, Aktuelle Aspekte des Mediums
Kunst*, Wilhelmspalais, Stuttgart, Alemania

1993
BT New Contemporaries, exposición itinerante (cat.)
Left Luggage, 10 Artists exposición itinerante
Matter and Fact, Collection Gallery, Londres,
Reino Unido (cat.)

1992
Invisible Cities, Fruitmarket Gallery, Edimburgo,
Reino Unido (cat.)
Three New Works, Transmission Gallery, Glasgow,
Reino Unido
Gesture No.5, Post West Gallery, Adelaide, Australia

1991
Museum Piece, instalación, Mackintosh Museum, Glasgow
School of Art, Reino Unido

BIBLIOGRAFÍA / BIBLIOGRAPHY

2010
Badia, Montse, *Recent History,* CAC Málaga - Tate St Ives
(cat. exp.)
Johnstone, Lesley, *Les Lendemains d'hier*, Musée d'art
contemporain de Montréal, 2010, p.122-127 (cat. exp.)

2009
Birnbaum, Daniel (ed.), *Making Worlds*, 53rd
International Art Exhibition. La Biennale di Venezia,
Venecia (cat. exp.)
Rosenberg, Angela; Heynen, Julian, *Under Lime Simon
Starling*, Temporäre Kunsthalle Berlin, Berlín (cat. exp.)
*Three Birds, Seven Stories, Interpolations and
Bifurcations*, Galleria Franco Noero, Turín, (cat. exp.)

2008
Alain Monsvoisin (ed), *Dictionnaire International
de la Sculpture Moderne & Contemporaine*, Edition
Du Regard, París
Cuttings [Supplement], The Power Plant, Toronto,
Canadá (cat. exp.)
Plant Room, Kunstraum Dornbirn, Dornbirn,
Austria (cat. exp.)
*The Greenroom: Reconsidering the Documentary and
Contemporary Art #1*, Sternberg Press Berlin and Center
for Curatorial Studies, Bard College, Annandale-on-Hudson
(cat. exp.)

2007

Feireiss, Lukas, *SPACECRAFT fleeting architecture and hideouts*, Berlín, p. 125

Held together with water, Kunst aus der Sammlung Verbund, MAK-Ausstellungshalle, Viena (cat. exp.)

Moscow Biennale of Contemporary Art, Moscú (cat. exp.)

Simon Starling - Nachbau, Museum Folkwang, Essen (cat. exp.)

2006

Szymczyk, Adam, *"Projections"*, *Le Temps*, 30.12.06, p. 44

Wittneven, Katrin, "Der Transformator", *Der Tagesspiegel*, 9.12.06, p. 28

Glauner, Max, "Skulptur mit Vorgeschichte", *zitty*, nº 25, 7.12.06

Maak, Niklas, "Das hysterische Flattern einer Segelyacht", *FAZ*, 2.12.06, p. 50

Müller, Katrin Bettina, "Flirt mit den Maschinen", *taz*, 29.11.06, p. 25

Hinrichsen, Jens, "Mechanisches Ballet", *artnet*, 28.11.06

Seele, Heide, "Ein Kunstwerk löscht sich selber aus", *Rhein-Neckar-Zeitung*, 24.11.06, p. 16

Strange I've Seen That Face Before, Städtisches Museum Abteiberg, Mönchengladbach, (cat. exp.)

24 hr. Tangenziale, Galleria Franco Noero, Turín (cat. exp.)

Drive. Cars in Contemporary Art, Galleria D'Arte Moderna, Bolonia (cat. exp.)

Robecchi, Michele, *Simon Starling*, *contemporary*, nº. 85, pp. 84-87

Bretton-Meyer, Henriette; Boyce, Martin; Starling, Simon, "Brain Mail: Some Thoughts On Ism Schism", *Neue Review*, enero, p. 10-14

2005

all Around all, BSI Art Collection Lugano, Lugano

Thomas, Gina, "Skurriler Erzähler", *Frankfurter Allgemeine Zeitung*, 7.12.05, p. 44

Menden, Alexander, "Erst Schuppen, dann Boot, dann wieder Schuppen", *Süddeutsche Zeitung*, 7.12.05, p. 15

universal experience. Art, Life and the Tourist's Eye, The Museum of Contemporary Art, Chicago (cat. exp.)

Higgins, Charlotte, "It's a shed, it's collapsible, it floats and (with help from a bike) it's the Winner", *The Guardian*, 6.12.05, p. 3

Jury, Louise, "Just an old bike? Or is it a poetic narrative? Either way, Starling flies to Turner Prize", *The Independent*, 6.12.05, p. 3

Alberge, Dalya, "One man and his boat shed sail into a storm over the Turner", *The Times*, 6.12.05, p. 3

Reynolds, Nigel, "Forget painting, Turner Prize is awarded to an old boatshed", *The Daily Telegraph*, 6.12.05

Reust, Hans Rudolf, "Simon Starling. Museum für Gegenwartskunst", *Artforum International*, octubre, pp. 285-286

Void Comix, nº 2, noviembre Searle, Adrian, "The house that Simon built (after sailing it a few miles down the Rhine)", *The Guardian*, 18.10.05, p. 4

Allen, Jennifer, "Ecologisch onderzoek en artistieke transformaties, Interview met Simon Starling", *Metropolis M*, nº 5, octubre-noviembre

Bradley, Will, "Objecten van Betekenis", *Metropolis M*, nº 5, octubre-noviembre

Pietsch, Hans, "Verwelkender Blumenstrauß", *art*, octubre, p. 145

Nicolaus, Frank y Bodtländer, Berndt, "Eine Schule des Wahnsinns", *art*, octubre, pp. 70-77

paralleles leben, Frankfurter Kunstverein Fráncfort (cat. exp.)

Hoffmann, Jens y Jonas, Joan, *Perform. Art Works*, Londres, pp. 68-69

Simon Starling. Cuttings, Kunstmuseum Basel, Museum für Gegenwart (cat.exp.)

Dean, Tacita y Millar, Jeremy, *Place*, Londres, pp. 52-53

DB, "Simon Starling. Museum für Gegenwartskunst", *Artforum International*, mayo, p. 138

Manacorda, Francesco, "Entropology. Monuments to Closed Systems", *Flash Art*, marzo-abril, pp. 76-79

Godfrey, Mark, "Image Structure", *Artforum International*, febrero, pp. 146-153

2004

Breuyne, Paul u.a., *Schöner Wohnen, kunst van heden voor alle dagen*, Bélgica

PART, Platform voor actuele kunst, Waregem (cat. exp.)

In the beginning there was the journey, 28 Bienal de Arte de Pontevedra, Pontevedra (cat. exp.)

Stange, Raimar, "Mehr oder Weniger", *spike*, octubre, p. 119

Jeffrey, Moira, "I want to ride my bicycle", *The Glasgow Herald*, 9.10.04

kbm, "Der Schwung", *tip*, 6-19.05.04, p. 8

Gioni, Massimiliano, "Simon Starling, the bricoleur", *Carnet,* abril-mayo, pp. 6-7

Starling, Simon & Manacorda, Francesco, *Simon Starling*, Villa Arson, Nice / Städtische Ausstellungshalle am Haverkamp, Münster (cat. exp.)

Birnbaum, Daniel, "Transporting Visions", *Artforum,* febrero, pp. 104-109

Volz, Jochen, *Turbulenz. Portikus Projekte 2001-2004*, Fráncfort, 2004

2003

Ehlers, Fiona, "Sieben Rhododendren reisen nach Hause", *Kultur Spiegel*, octubre, pp. 16-21

Barak, Ami, "Gegeben sei: Die Leuchtlampe", *Skulptur Biennale Münsterland*, Münster, modo Verlag (cat. exp.)

Fox, Dan, "50th Venice Biennale. Review", *Frieze*, septiembre, pp. 100-101

Vetrocq, Marcia E., "Venice Biennale: Every Idea But One", *Art in America*, septiembre, pp. 76-87

Dunn, Melissa, "The Venice Biennale: Slouching Toward Utopia", *Flash Art*, julio-septiembre, pp. 47 y 54

Lorch, Catrin, "La Biennale di Venezia", *Kunst-Bulletin*, julio-agosto, pp. 22-27

Selvaratnam, Troy, "The Starling Variations", *Parkett*, nº 67, pp. 6-14

Stange, Raimar; Perrella, Cristiana; Maraniello, Gianfranco, *Simon Starling*, Museo d'Arte Contemporanea Roma, Mondadori Electa (cat. exp.)

Brevi, Manuela, "Arte eventi", *Arte*, junio, p. 42

Vanderbilt, Tom, "A Thousand Words", *Artforum,* mayo, pp. 140-141

Menin, Samuele und Sansone, Valentina; "Sculpture Forever. Contemporary Sculpture (Part I)", *Flash Art*, mayo-junio, pp. 122-129

Millner, Jaqueline; *Mathew Jones,* "+ Simon Starling", *Broadsheet*, diciembre 2002 / enero-febrero 2003

2002

Tufnell, Rob, *Flaga (1972-2000)*, Galleria Franco Noero, Turín (cat. exp.)

Römer, Stefan, "Zusammenbiegen, was das Zeug hält", *Texte zur Kunst*, nº 48, diciembre

Hill, Peter, *Double Vision*, "The Sydney Morning Herald", 25.10.02

Low, Lenny Ann, "Mathew Jones/Simon Starling", *The Sydney Morning Herald Metropolitan*, 19.10.02

Kyriacou, Sotiris, "Mathew Jones / Simon Starling", *Contemporary*, septiembre, p. 12

"Mathew Jones / Simon Starling", *Skylines*, septiembre-octubre, p. 36

Storer, Russell; Bretton-Meyer, Henriette, *Jones /Starling*, Museum of Contemporary Art, Sídney (cat. exp.)

Danicke, Sandra, "Cereus, Kaktus aus Spanien", *Neue Züricher Zeitung*, 4.10.02, p. 58

"'Kakteenhaus' von Simon Starling im Portikus", *Frankfurter Allgemeine Zeitung*, 14.09.02

Hohmann, Silke, "Die Überlegenheit des Umwegs", *Frankfurter Rundschau*, 14.09.02

Volz, Jochen, *Kakteenhaus*, Portikus, Fráncfort (cat. exp.)

Schöne, Veronica, "Diät im Kontext", *Szene Hamburg*, agosto, pp. 62-63

Keil, Frank, "Schwimmtofu an Schweineporträt", *Frankfurter Rundschau,* 7.08.02

Büsing, Nicole y Klaas, Heiko, "West-östliche Vereinigung", *Kieler Nachrichten*, 2.07.02

Schellen, Petra, "Nach dem Müll-Clash", *TAZ* (edición de Hamburgo), 1.07.02

Gardner, Belinda Grace, "Die Tiere beten jeden Tag zum lieben Tofu", *Die Welt* (edición de Hamburgo), 1.07.02

Gebbers, Anna-Catharina, "Zusammenhänge herstellen", *Artist Kunstmagazin*, marzo

Schöne, Veronika, *Zusammenhänge herstellen*, Kunstverein in Hamburg (cat. exp.)

Leffingwell, Edward, "Simon Starling at Casey Kaplan", *Art in America*, julio

Wilson, Michael, "Artforum Picks: Simon Starling", *www. artforum.com*, marzo

Burton, Johanna, "Simon Starling", *Time Out New York*, 21-28 marzo, nº 338

"Art Reviews: Simon Straling", *The New Yorker*, 18.03.02

Levin, Kim, "Voice Choices: Simon Starling", *The Village Voice*, 13.03.02

Brown, Katarina M., *Djungel*, Dundee Contemporary Arts, Dundee (cat. exp.)

2001

Price, Elizabeth, *Small Gold Medal*, Londres: Book Works
Asthoff, Jens, "Simon Starling", *artist Kunstmagazin*,
nº 4/2001, pp. 4-7
Jens Asthoff, "Simon Starling im Kunstverein",
Kunstbulletin, octubre, p. 35
Angela Rosenberg, "Variations On A Theme", *Flash Art*,
julio-septiembre, nº 219, pp. 100-102
"Here + Now, Scottish Art 1990-2001", Dundee
Contemporary Arts, Dundee, p. 122 (cat. exp.)
MacKenna, Deirdre; Tufnell, Rob; Starling, Simon,
Poul Henningsen. Simon Starling, Cooper Gallery,
University of Dundee, Dundee (cat. exp.)
Simon Starling CMYK / RGB, FRAC Languedoc Roussillon,
Montpellier (cat. exp.)
Millar, Jeremy, *Inverted Retrograde Theme*; Wiener
Secession, Viena (cat. exp.)
Weinrautner, Ina, "Werke mit doppeltem Boden",
Handelsblatt; 3.05.01, nº 85, p. 52
Ebner, Jörn, "Briten landen in Berlin", *Frankfurter
Allgemeine Zeitung*, 5.05.01, nº 104, p. 53
Stange, Raimar, "Public Relations", *Kunstbulletin*, mayo,
nº 5, pp. 20-25
McKee, Francis, "Chicken or Egg?", *Frieze*, enero-febrero,
nº 56, pp. 74-78

2000

Griese, Horst, "Umwege machen das Leben interessanter",
Weser Kurier, 7.12.00, nº 286
Engberg, Juliana, *Simon Starling*, Camden Arts Center
London, Londres (cat. exp.)
Meyric Hughes, Henry, "Manifesta", *tema celeste -
Contemporary Art Magazine*, octubre-diciembre,
pp. 102-103
Paulli, Luca, "A Project for a Space", *tema celeste - Contempo-
rary Art Magazine; http: // www. temaceleste.com*, marzo
Schultz, Deborah, "The Office of Misplaced Events
(Temporary Annex)", *Art Monthly*, enero, pp. 31-32

1999

Shepheard, Paul, "Edgeless, Modeless", Context, *Afterall*,
nº 1, Londres, pp. 101-104
Esche, Charles, "Undomesticating Modernism", Text,
Afterall, nº 1, pp. 90-100

Bradley, Will, *Project for a Modern Museum*, Moderna
Museet, Estocolmo (cat. exp.)
Esche, Charles; Starling, Simon; Sembill, Stefanie y
Winkelmann, Jan, *Simon Starling*, Galerie für
Zeitgenössische Kunst, Leipzig (cat. exp.)
"Leipziger Premiere fürs Palermo-Stipendium", *Leipziger
Volkszeitung*, 11.01.99
Tazaki, Anni L., "Ready-Made made-ready", *Flyer*, nº 5
"Blinky Palermo", Stipendium, *Bild*, 12.01.99
Kowa, Günter, "Der wundersame Fischzug mit der
Museumsvitrine", *Mitteldeutsche Zeitung*, 6.04.99

1998

Sommer, Tim, "Vieldeutiges Spiel um Erinnerungen",
Leipziger Volkszeitung, 8.04.99
Sinclair, Ross, "Blue Boat Black", *Frieze*, febrero
Sachs, Hinrich, *Double Narrative (after Robert Smithson)*;
The Modern Institute, Glasgow (cat. exp.)
Reconstructions, Smart Project Space, Ámsterdam (cat.exp.)

1997

Loock, Ulrich, *Transference*, Glasgow / Kunsthalle Bern
(cat. exp.)
McKee, Francis, *Blue Boat Black*, Transmission Gallery
(cat. exp.)
Sinclair, Ross, "Simon Starling", *Frieze*, nº 38

1996

Feldmann, Melissa, "Matters of Fact, New Conceptualism
in Scotland", *Third Text 37*, invierno 96-97, pp. 75-84

1995

Morgan, Stuart, "The future's not what it used to be",
Frieze, marzo-abril
Hunt, Ian, "Simon Starling, The Showroom, London",
Frieze, septiembre-octubre
Jaio, Miren, "Simon Starling, The Showroom, London",
Lápiz, nº 115
Currah, Mark, "Showroom", *Time Out*, julio

1991

Palmer, Roger, "There is no museum in the exhibition at
present", *Alba*, julio

Este catálogo se publica con motivo de la exposición *Simon Starling. Recent History*
en el CAC Málaga (26 noviembre 2010 - 23 enero 2011) y en la Tate St Ives (5 febrero - 2 mayo 2011) /
This book was published on the occasion of the exhibition *Simon Starling. Recent History*
CAC Málaga (26 November 2010 - 23 January 2011) and Tate St Ives (5 February - 2 May 2011)

CAC MÁLAGA

Alemania s/n
29001 Málaga
T +34 952 12 00 55. F +34 952 21 01 77
http://www.cacmalaga.org

Fernando Francés
Director

Mª José García
Gerencia / Manager

Alicia Bustamante
Administración / Administration

Almudena Bocanegra
Adjunta Dirección / Directorial Assistant

Helena Juncosa, Covadonga Hernández
Exposiciones / Exhibitions

Victoria Ruiz, Oana Stroe
Actividades Culturales / Cultural Activities

Elena Padrón, Alberto Ricca, Mercedes Almagro
Comunicación e Imagen / Comunication & Design

Inés Fernández, Pilar Díaz, Celia García
Actividades Pedagógicas / Education

AYUNTAMIENTO DE MÁLAGA / MÁLAGA CITY COUNCIL

Francisco de la Torre Prados
Alcalde / Mayor

Miguel Briones
Delegado de Cultura / Cultural Delegate

José Óscar Carrascosa
Director General de Cultura, Educación y Fiestas / General Director of Culture

Javier Ferrer
Gerente / Manager

María Teresa Barrau
Secretaria de la Comisión / Registrar Comission

EXPOSICIÓN / EXHIBITION CAC MÁLAGA

Fernando Francés
Comisario / Curator

Helena Juncosa, Gestión Cultural y Comunicación, S. L.
Organización y Coordinación / Organization and Coordination

TDM. Transportes y Montajes de Arte, S. L.
Transporte / Transport

Ferrer & Ojeda Asociados
Seguro / Insurance

Mihail E. Plesanu, Fernando Sarria, Jan Dunkel, Jan Bleicher
Montaje / Installation

British Council
Colaborador / Supporter

TATE ST IVES

Porthmeor Beach, St Ives
Cornwall TR26 1TG
T +44 (0)1736 796226. F +44 (0)1736 793794
http://www.tate.org.uk/stives

Martin Clark
Director Artístico y comisario / Artistic Director and Curator

Mark Osterfield
Director Ejecutivo / Executive Director

Sara Hughes
Comisaria / Curator

Matthew McDonald
Registro / Registrar

Alex Lambley
Responsable de Comunicación / Communications Manager

Arwen Fitch
Departamento de Prensa / Press Officer

Susan Lamb
Responsable de Educación / Head of Learning

Simon Pollard
Jefe Técnico / Senior Technician

Jowdy Davey
Departamento de Desarrollo / Development Officer

**Tate St Ives Members
Tate Members
The Henry Moore Foundation**
Colaboradores / The Simon Starling Exhibition Supporter Group

CATÁLOGO / PUBLICATION

Fernando Francés, Martin Clark, Montse Badia
Textos / Texts

Alberto Ricca
Diseño / Design

Laura E. Suffield, Discobole, S. L.
Traducción / Translation

Kasper Akhøj, Ruth Clark, Marc Domage, José Luis Gutiérrez, Aurélien Mole, Anders Sune Berg, Cary Whittier, Jens Ziehe
Fotografía / Photo Credits

Imprenta Cervantina, S. L.
Impresión / Printer

ISBN: 978-84-96159-91-4
Depósito Legal: MA-2082-2010

AGRADECIMIENTOS / ACKNOWLEDGMENTS

Valerie Chartrain, Pierpaolo Falone, Uffe Holm, Carolina Kirsop, Maria Elisa Marchini, Tim Neuger, Franco Noero, Burkhard Riemschneider, Valeria Riva

Galleria Franco Noero, Turín; neugerriemschneider, Berlín; The Modern Institute, Glasgow; Casey Kaplan, Nueva York; Filmprojektion Mondt, Hamburgo

Nuestro agradecimiento muy especial a Simon Starling sin cuyo apoyo, implicación y entusiasmo esta exposición no hubiera sido posible / Especially to Simon Starling without whose support and enthusiasm this exhibition would not have been possible

BRITISH COUNCIL

The Henry Moore
Foundation